THE STENCIL COLLECTION

THE STENCIL COLLECTION

JOCASTA INNES

and

STEWART WALTON

Paintability

AURUM PRESS

For Debenie

First published 1995 by Aurum Press Ltd,
25 Bedford Avenue, London WC1B 3AT

2 4 6 8 10 9 7 5 3 1
1996 1998 1999 1997 1995
Introductory pages and endmatter © Paintability 1995
All other matter © Paintability 1990, 1995

Stencil design by Stewart Walton
Colourwash crackle glaze kits by Jocasta Innes/Housestyle
Art direction, production and design by Photograft
Introduction designed by Don Macpherson
Introduction photography by Graham Rae
Location photography by James Merrell
Studio photography by Tino Tedaldi
Styling by Karina Garrick
Stencilling by Matthew Usmar Lauder

Original Morris designs kindly loaned by William Morris
Gallery, Lloyd Park, Forest Road, London E17. The authors and
publisher wish to thank Norah Gillow of the William Morris Gallery.

Hand-painted silk flowers in the Textiles Collection
by Maxine Hoff,
87 Black Lion Lane, London W6.
Beige and white striped fabric by Sanderson.

Tartan Dining Room stencil design by Stewart Walton and John Crummay.

A catalogue record for this book is available from the British Library

ISBN 1 85410 366 0

CONTENTS

THE STENCIL STORY

Stencils are probably one of the most ancient of decorative tools, a short cut to repeat-pattern making that has been in use since the time of the Pharaohs. While the master painter worked on his mural subjects freehand, a team of apprentices could be left to get on with stencilling all the repeating elements of the design, from papyrus fronds to patterned borders. In medieval churches they would be stencilling gold stars on the ceilings. The fact is, no one need be afraid of trying their hand at stencilling. No guess work is involved, only a readiness to follow instructions, to experiment with colour and different techniques, and to practise a few routines on paper beforehand.

This is not to say that the results cannot be spectacular. Imagine the walls of a garden room dripping with stencilled wisteria; a dark hallway studded with gold stars; an attic bedroom strewn with violets; a painted floor featuring its own stencilled kilim-style rug in all the glowing colours you have ever coveted. The fashion now is for stencilling on a generous scale, more like a hand-printed wallpaper than the tiny borders we all started out with a few years ago. Of course, this takes time. However, you do not have to complete a project over the weekend and, anyway, it is hard to begrudge the time when the transformation keeps growing under your eyes. Stencils, along with the colour excitement they bring, definitely help stamp your own personality on your surroundings.

If a whole room seems daunting, start with something smaller, a chest of drawers, maybe, or a bath surround, or kitchen-unit doors. Take trouble over the preparation, varnish the finished work conscientiously, and you will be delighted with the professional look of the end result.

This book wraps up a collection of stencils that has been growing over many years: floral classics, feisty ethnic patterns, a selection of favourite motifs based on designs by one of the legendary pattern makers, William Morris. But where it scores most strongly is in the wealth of practical step-by-step illustrations, showing what tools and colours to use; short-cuts that produce exciting results; tips on extending, reversing or combining different pattern elements for different surfaces and on varying scales. There are ideas for stencilling on fabrics, creating stencilled cushions, and transforming inexpensive calico or hessian into something quite special. There are tips you will want to experiment with — stencilling with sponges, for instance, or using transparent colour for the charmingly faded tints of an antique patchwork quilt.

Stencilling is a craft, or hobby, to have fun with. In fact, it's a good idea to invite a friend round to lend a hand, on the understanding, of course, that you return the compliment. Getting started is always a problem when you are embarking on an unfamiliar routine. Having someone there to bounce ideas off, and share the tea-breaks with, always makes the project seem twice as much fun and half as problematic.

One word of advice. We do not any-where advocate using spray paints for stencilling. Professional stencillers get excellent results with these, but they require expert handling, the fumes are seriously toxic and what they save in muscle power they lose in time spent masking off, covering floors and furniture. Stencilling the old-fashioned way (but using fast-drying modern paints) looks every bit as good, and is a tidy, small-scale operation, which you can get back to as and when convenient. Do not rush out and buy a load of equipment, either. A basic kit of paint colours, two or three brushes, paper plates for mixing on, rags, empty jars, and a really sturdy, light, folding stepladder are all you need, except for a stencil card and a knife, etc. for cutting your own stencil. An apron with large pockets to stuff extra brushes in, and rags for wiping off the odd splash or smear are useful too.

Colour is a personal thing. We have shown a wide range of colour possibilities in this book, but they are only suggestions, so do not feel obliged to stick with them. If you like the shape or style of a particular motif, but not the colours, try to imagine it in a completely different colourway. Gold paisley motifs on a dark-green or blue base could look sumptuous; convolvulus in tones of blue on a white background might be fresh and pretty in a small bathroom. The options are endless, literally, which is one of the reasons why stencilling continues to appeal to each new generation of homeowners. All the ready-pasted wallpapers and one-coat paints cannot compare for satisfaction with the glow that comes of dreaming up a transformation and seeing it evolve, through your own hands and skill, into your own personal creation. But watch out. As word gets round, you could find that what started out as a sudden impulse grows into a full-time job. It has been known.

These are designs which are complete in themselves, for example, a large spot motif or a cluster of fruit with leaves and stems. They can be used singly, to emphasise painted furniture, or repeated on a grid for a dramatic 'wallpaper' effect.

STENCIL TYPES

If you look through the range of stencils in this book you will find that they fall into one of three categories, which are described here.

Borders

Most beginners like to start with borders, using them as a visual trim around ceilings, above skirtings, to outline door frames, or at dado-height, to break up walls that look too high for the floor area. Our border stencils are designed so that the end of one section dovetails into the start of the next. Borders can look particularly attractive if you use two, one beneath the other, for a deeper ornamental band.

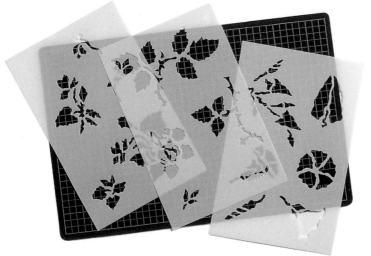

Modular Stencils

These motifs are used together to create a free-flowing, non-repeating design, like a growing plant. The Woodbine in this book is a good example. Once you get the hang of modular stencils, you will find that you can use them to achieve artistic effects similar to freehand mural painting. Other examples include leaf trails and single sprays of flowers, etc. These are used for linking motifs, to balance a shape, to fill a space more effectively, or simply to vary a repeat motif.

All the stencil designs used in the projects are printed together at the end of this book. Rather than cutting them out, try photocopying them; first keep them the same size as shown, then enlarge or reduce as necessary. Alternatively, trace them off using architects' tracing paper, which comes in rolls. Use a black felt-tip pen for a firm outline.

CUTTING YOUR STENCIL

In the past people used all sorts of materials to make their stencils, including oiled parchment, leather and zinc sheets. Parchment and leather were lighter to transport — a real advantage for an itinerant stenciller who travelled with his equipment on his back, or in his saddle bags. On the other hand, a sheet of thin metal such as zinc (soft enough to cut, yet heavy enough to lie flat to the wall) had the advantage of durability, particularly useful when the stencilled decoration was on a large scale, for instance covering the walls of a Victorian polychrome church.

These days most stencillers choose stencil card (an oiled card) or transparent mylar (a thin plastic sheet) for cutting their stencils. Card is not so durable as mylar, though brushing on a thin PVA solution before use helps seal the cut edges. It is, however, easier to cut smoothly. Mylar has the toughness of plastic in its favour, and is transparent (though this is lost as you paint over it), but it is tricky to cut and has a tendency to split unless handled carefully.

Cutting Procedure: If you have chosen stencil card, begin by lightly spraying the back of the design, then stick it down on the card, smoothing it out as you do so. If using mylar, spray the front of the design and attach it below the mylar sheet so the design shows through.

Cutting Tips: Try to cut in a single fluent stroke, turning the stencil round rather than changing your cutting position. This smooth, confident cutting comes with practice. Try it, and you will soon find yourself falling into a comfortable rhythm. Change your blades frequently — a keen blade makes all the difference. Keep your left hand, if you are right-handed, on the side opposite your cut (or vice

Next lay your card or mylar on a cutting mat, which is a worthwhile investment as it allows you to cut over and over again on a nicely cushioned surface, and the cuts 'heal' again after use. The best cutting tool is a craft knife or scalpel, with a good supply of sharp new blades. You may need pliers to help extract or insert blades safely.

versa, if left-handed). When cutting card, try to hold your knife at an angle, to give a bevelled edge to the cut. This not only looks more professional, but helps prevent paint creeping underneath. Don't worry too much about tears or slips of the knife. These can be repaired with tiny strips of masking-tape, or sellotape, applied band-aid fashion across the tear. Trim off any excess tape with your knife.

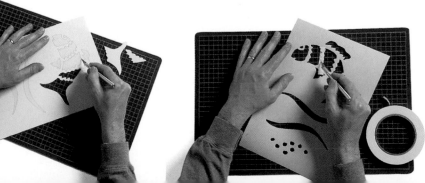

BRUSHES, SPONGES AND PAINTS

Brushes and Sponges

Most stencillers like to keep a selection of brushes to choose from, though there is no need to buy them all at once. It is a matter of horses for courses.

Good-quality artists' fitches, with filbert tips, are pleasant to use, though their long handles can get in the way (you can saw these down).

Round-headed, mop-style stencil brushes, made with bristle, are suitable for most work, and come in several sizes. They are used in a circular scrubbing action, with the minimum of paint (a *golden rule* when stencilling); this is a less tiring way of working over a large area.

Blunt-cut stencil brushes (the traditional type) are useful for stippling fine detail cleanly, but are tiring to use over large areas. (The neck and arm really feel it!)

Avoid cheap brushes as they shed bristles. Ragged tips can be tidied by snipping carefully with sharp scissors. Also avoid synthetic brushes, which do not retain paint well. Do not use standard paintbrushes, either; they are the wrong shape.

Sponges are fun to use for a broken-colour, textured effect. They also produce rapid results, and you will find that the work zips along. Practise first on paper, though, to get the feel of a sponge, and do not pick up too much paint. Natural sponges, with their varied textures, give the most attractive prints, on the whole. But try a synthetic sponge, too — you may like the closer texture. Cut the sponge if it overlaps the stencil too much.

Paints

Artists' acrylic colours (mostly available in tubes, although larger sizes come in squeezy bottles) are the ideal stencilling medium because they dry so quickly and, once dry, are waterproof. They can be used straight from the tube, for total cover, or thinned with water, for a more sensitive transparent effect. You can make this still more attractive by adding a very little flow enhancer (available from art shops) to the mix on your plate, but test first on paper.

Standard (latex) emulsions used in the home are quite adequate for stencilling and you may wish to work with these if you have some left over. However, they 'build' quickly, clogging the stencils, and can look too thick unless handled deftly. Swatch-pot sizes are generally available. The colours can all be mixed, and further tinted with acrylics.

A touch of gold — or silver, or copper, there are lots of metallic shades available — can do wonders for a stencilled pattern, highlighting a motif or adding subdued richness to a border. But remember not to overdo it; splashing on gold paint can produce a garish effect. Metallic waxes, rubbed on with a fingertip, give a soft touch of brilliance. These come in many shades, and a jar lasts a long time.

Fabric stencil paints are a new addition to the stenciller's kit, especially now that customising inexpensive fabrics — calico, muslin, cotton duck — is so fashionable. The latest fabric stencil paints are flexible enough to hang well, and are washable.

There are many ranges of stencil paints on offer; it is cheaper to buy these in small containers. Try one or two colours to see whether you like the consistency. Be careful not to let them become either sticky or too watery.

A small stencil can usually be held with your free hand while you work, but large stencils are best held in place with either a light squirt of spray mount across the back, or with tabs of masking tape at the corners. Spray mount is especially helpful for very open work such as lacy stencils, which can be pressed flat and tight to the wall as you paint, leaving your hands free. The stencil can also be peeled off again and re-used. But do not overdo the spray mount and do not inhale the fumes.

Squeeze, pour or spoon (use plastic spoons) a little of your paint colour onto your plate. Waxed-paper plates (the type used for picnics and parties) make excellent disposable palettes.

Dip the tip of your brush in the paint and stipple onto newspaper. This blots up moisture while drawing colour up into the bristles to load the brush. Practise with a stencil on clean paper. If colour leaks under the stencil, or if you find a rim forming round the outer edges, your brush is overloaded. If the colour splats so that the design is blurred, your brush is too wet. Keep pouncing the brush on paper until the colour is crisp and delicate; for beginners, the moment when the brush seems too dry to work is usually when stencilling should begin. Also remember to wipe the back of the stencil frequently with a soft rag.

Brush and Sponge Techniques

Stippling, using a blunt-cut traditional brush, gives a slower build-up of colour and is tiring to do, but offers considerable control. To stipple, pounce the bristle tips firmly onto the surface through the stencil. Use a small brush for small detail.

Using a soft rounded brush in a circular motion gives fast results, suited to bold motifs. But it is essential not to overload the brush, and to pounce off the moisture first. Test and practise.

Brushing in one direction throughout can help to pick up the shape interestingly — as in the photograph below, where it emphasises the scales and curves of the fish motif. This technique can add dynamism, but remember — use a nearly dry brush or the paint will build up messily along the right-hand cuts.

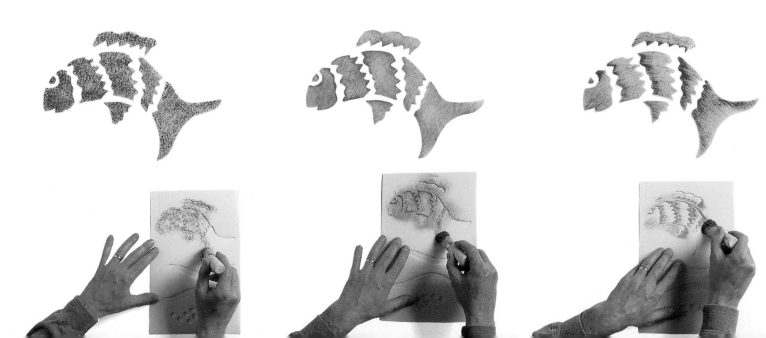

It is easy, at first, to get hung up on the rules, to worry too much about the right way and wrong way to work. But half the fun and creativity of applying design via stencils comes from 'playing' with your image. The old stencillers were adept at this, getting a lot more mileage out of

A simple border, repeated, can give a rich and interesting striped wallpaper effect. This involves a lot of work (though less on furniture) but the result is entirely your own thing.

Simpler still, try a mirror image for a satisfyingly balanced composition. To do this, just turn your stencil over and work from the back.

HOW TO STENCIL

their basic library of motifs. If a motif looks skinny and needs fattening up, try adding a leaf here and there from another design, or a border to frame it, or use one of the simple tricks shown above.

The easiest way to apply shading is to use a slightly darker tone of the base colour as shown below, applying it sparingly, just for emphasis and not necessarily to give a three-dimensional effect.

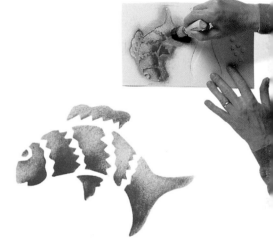

A sponged stencil gains interest from the open texture of the sponge, giving a pointillist look to the design. Sponging is fast and fun, and especially effective when used on a large-scale architectural design. It softens a hard-edged motif attractively.

Going over a motif with a darker shade or a different shade altogether adds richness and artistic complexity. Do not apply the second colour throughout the design, just here and there. Colours need not be naturalistic — try using crimson shading on an orange crab apple, for instance, or maybe a touch of green or brown. Experiment!

Blending colours is usually a matter of gentle and sparing stippling with the second colour, producing a richer, softly rounded look.

Marking Out Walls

Everyone finds this tedious, but the equipment needed is minimal: a plumb line, a spirit level, maybe a wooden batten, and a stick of chalk or a pencil. Conscientiously done, this will give your work a thoroughly professional finish.

A plumb line — it could be a weight on a length of string with a tack to hold it in place — is essential to find the true vertical on walls. But be sensible; wonky walls may call for a little adjustment, especially if floors and ceilings are also out of true. Trust your eye, too.

The string from your plumb line or a strip of Low Tack masking tape will keep you on the straight and narrow.

Preparation and Finishing Up

Any bare wood surface should be smoothed and cleaned up before stencilling. Use medium- to fine-grade abrasive paper, and work in the direction of the grain, firmly but gently. Then wipe down with a damp rag.

When stencilling on fabric, make sure this is smoothly ironed first. Lay it out flat on a wide surface, maybe a kitchen table, protected with sheets of paper. Stretch out the fabric and pin here and there before slipping a sheet of clean card underneath. Do this before stencilling as fabric paint will tend to seep through.

Use a good-size spirit level to find the true horizontal and make little pencil or chalk marks as a guide.

A stencilled design is a labour of love, and needs protection, especially if it is on a surface that will take a beating. Use a matt, oil-based or polyurethane varnish on walls, diluted with a little appropriate solvent. On furniture use a semi-gloss, but apply two to three coats, sanding each coat when dry for a silky feel.

Look After Your Stencils

Anyone who has gone through the labour of transferring and hand-cutting their own stencils should need no reminding that these are precious things, too valuable to discard or mistreat. It only takes a minute to clean up stencils as well as brushes at the end of a session, and the effort will pay off when you have built up your own stencil library, to which you can refer at any time.

Card stencils should be wiped down with a damp, clean rag. It is always sensible to stencil your first cut-out straight onto a spare sheet of card, though, because card stencils do not last for ever. Mylar is tougher, and can be cleaned by soaking for a while in hot soapy water and then scrubbing down with a soft (but not too soft) brush to remove traces of dry paint.

The
Woodbine
Parlour

The
Woodbine
Parlour

A twist of stem unites three arrowy leaf shapes, which form one repeating element in our Woodbine stencil.

A variant of the **stem and leaf** theme with more of a suggestion of the clinging tendrilly habit of growth.

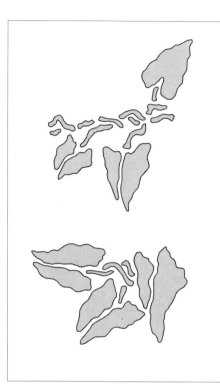

One of the incidental pleasures of this Country Lane Collection is being able to get a closer look at some of the exquisite miniatures that can get lost in the profusion of summer growth.

BINDING ARTISTRY

or How to Tame a Creeper Without Getting in a Tangle

Woodbine, with its fragile trumpet flowers delicately striped with pink, is one of the most fleeting of wild flowers, no sooner picked than withered. Translated into a stencil, its transient beauty is fixed for ever.

A single leaf can be used to add emphasis where your design needs it.

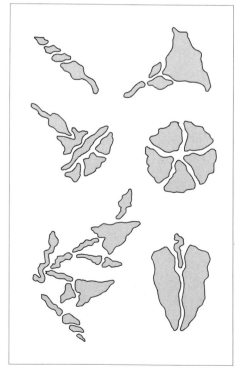

Four versions of the characteristic **Woodbine flower**, from tightly furled bud to a fully opened flower. Keep alternating these for a lively naturalistic effect.

The growing tip of a Woodbine stem has smaller leaves and buds, and clinging, spiralling tendrils.

1 Using a clear mid-green, stencil a leaf cluster, taking care not to overload your brush. It is far better that you make the colour too light at first — it can always be deepened later on. Wait until the paint has dried before making any adjustments because dry colour is always lighter.

2 Leaves as expressive as the ones that make up the Woodbine stencil gain enormously from shading here and there in different tones of green. Arrive at these by adding a little blue (for a cooler green) or raw umber (for a softer green) to your original colour. To shade, stipple colour on very lightly with a soft but firm bristled brush.

CLIMBING ART

ADD Twiddly tendrils reaching out for new supports are a very characteristic Woodbine feature, and this makes it easy to extend the design and give a sense of the plant's eagerly climbing growth. The twining growth makes it easy to extend or develop your stencilling in any direction, to suit your own room scheme and features.

FILL OUT 'Horses for courses' also applies to stencils; to fill a squarer space the elements need to be grouped together more compactly, as shown here. Try to keep a balance of colour between flowers and leaves for the most attractive effect.

3 Flowers can be stencilled in wherever they look right, once you have established the framework of Woodbine leaves and twining stems. Woodbine flowers belong to the Ipomea family, which include Morning Glories, so you can take your pick of colours from pure white, pink and white, or heavenly blue. Here we used pale, clear pink.

4 A profile view of the same flower added to the previous cluster is starting to build up a shapely motif. Petals can be shaded lightly with clear yellow green, as here, or add a pistachio green dot by hand in the centre of the petals.

BUILD Your stencilled Woodbine grows like the real thing, putting out new leading shoots and exploring tendrils. If you repeat the previous flowering group, you will begin to create a positive but informal and lively border. Our picture above shows the design both curved round into wreaths, and stencilled vertically as a border.

19

Wild flowers seem to look more at home on an airy and casual-looking painted finish. Here we have used a clear yellow colourwash applied over a white emulsion base, to give a soft but sunny emphasis, especially valuable in dark or north-facing rooms.

NATURE ALL ENTWIN'D

Where to put your stencils is one of the first decisions to be made. They can be as symmetrical or as free-form as you choose. This low-ceilinged cottage room, with its odd little nooks and features, seems to call for an informal stencil treatment. Woodbine wanders prettily around a white painted plank door and up either side of a beam. Further tendrils encircling a plain card lampshade pick up the floral theme attractively. In a more conventional space, you might prefer to use the stencils more architecturally, underlining a cornice, or perhaps decorating the panels of a door. This would give a more composed effect.

Internal shutters, painted and stencilled, make an unusual and practical alternative to curtains at a small cottage window. In the daytime they can be folded right back to admit as much light as possible but, closed at night, the stencilled decoration comes into its own and gives a finished and cosy appearance, as well as keeping out the draughts. The Woodbine motif would look equally pretty stencilled on to a heavy cotton curtain, as a border design.

Shutters like these are a fairly simple DIY job: rectangles of sturdy plywood, with a flat moulding glued around the edges. Protect stencilled design with two coats of clear matt varnish.

A really junky firescreen can still be picked up for a pound or so in a jumble sale, and will look stunning when painted and stencilled to tone with your decor. Here, it gets a new lease of life with a background of soft yellow, and a stencilled wreath of flowering Woodbine.

NEW GROWTH ON OLD WOOD

It's Attention to Detail that Makes the Difference

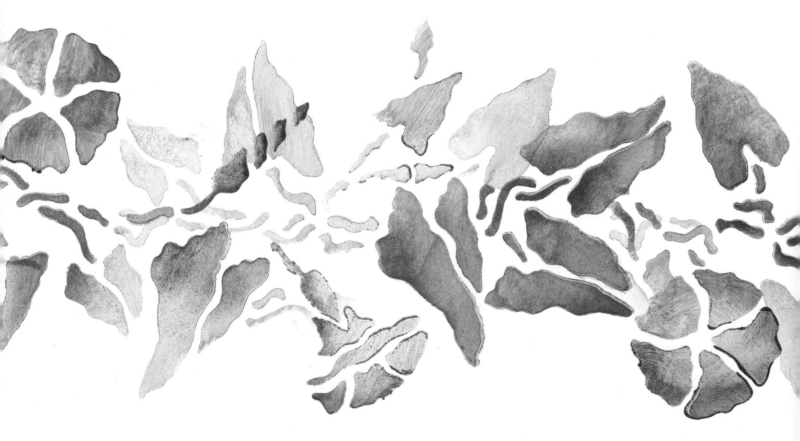

Although we have chosen pretty, naturalistic colours for our Country Lanes stencils, this is only a starting point, and there is no reason why you should not experiment with the same designs in much bolder, 'fantasy' colours, as here. This is especially true of the Woodbine design, where the stencilled shapes are strong and distinctive enough to carry a more dramatic colour scheme.

To show what a difference a change of colour scheme makes, we decorated this useful tray table in a pretty blue-green Crackleglaze. The striking texture of the crackled finish makes an unexpected background to the stencilled decoration, adding piquancy to a pink and white colour scheme which might otherwise have been too sweet. Choose a strong background colour to provide a good contrast through the lighter, crackled topcoat. This is not a subtle effect, so be brave when choosing the colours.

The
Violet
Bedroom

The
Violet
Bedroom

Our main **Violet** stencil has something of the charm of an illustration in an Elizabethan herbal. It can either be used on its own as a design unit, or combined with the smaller elements below.

These little **Violet buds** interspersed with the main stencil give a spriggy Victorian look, or used on their own are a delicate decoration for small accessories.

Violet plants have the perfection of miniatures, and are special in that every part of the plant — delicate flowers and buds and tiny heart-shaped leaves — is equally decorative.

VIOLETS ARE BLUE

or How to Gather a Painted Posy

Scattered demurely over beamed and whitewashed walls, and adorning a lacy pillowslip, our Violet stencil has the irresistible prettiness of an old Valentine.

Different views of **flowering Violet** plants add variety to the basic stencil theme.

Small **linking elements** are used when stencilling Violets as a continuous border, between the main stencils.

1 Mix medium green for the leaves and stem of the main Violet stencil, and brush it through the stencil using a firm bristled brush with a light stippling movement for the cleanest impression. Neatness matters more with delicate shapes like these.

THE ART OF FLOWERS

ISOLATE If you only want to use one small stencil element, as here, simply take a little more care when stencilling.

BUILD Adding smaller elements each side of the main Violet stencil creates a completely different shape, which would sit well on a chair back or a bedhead.

2 With a slightly darker shade of green, stipple over some areas of the leaves to give a sense of movement, and emphasise the stems. You may find it useful to use a finer brush for stencilling the stems and tendrils.

3 Use more than one shade of mauve, from pale violet to purple, to bring out the character and form of the Violet flowers. Too pale colours may tend to lose definition.

COMPOSE This pretty informal grouping of stencil elements makes up a unit which can be used as it stands or repeated indefinitely to create a continuous border with a pleasantly irregular and asymmetric movement to it. Violets grow randomly by sending out runners with new plants at their tip, so creating a naturalistic border is easy.

The attractively irregular walls and beams in this cottage bedroom seem to call for a more relaxed use of pattern than a grander room. Instead of being carefully placed in a regular grid pattern (which gives quite a different effect — and takes much longer) all the stencil elements have been used here in an almost haphazard scattering, as if the window had opened and blown violets all over the room.

EVERYTHING'S COMING UP VIOLETS

Picking up the theme more formally, a parterre of Violets edges a canvas floor cloth, a wreath of tiny buds circles the lampshade, and one perfect plant adorns a prized pillowcase.

HOW DOES YOUR GARDEN GROW?

It's Attention to Detail that Makes the Difference

*A posy of ideas to inspire you to use
your Violet stencils in all sorts of
fresh and attractive ways. Half the
fun of stencilling is adding the little
decorative details, which only take
a minute or so, but give the finished
room such a thoughtfully
composed look.*

Encircling inexpensive
card lampshades, and
detailing the corners of a painted
bedside table; two more ideas for
getting the best from your Violet
stencil set. When stencilling on
furniture, be sure to finish the
process by sealing with one or two
coats of matt varnish.

This informal composition is achieved by using transparent watercolours with varying intensity, and overlapping stencil elements.

A Violet border makes something very special of a simple painted canvas floorcloth. A variant might be to stencil Violet posies in a lighter colour on a dark painted background.

Airy drifts of translucent muslin make a delightful sheer background for a scattering of stencilled Violets. People are often nervous of stencilling on to fabric, but it is just as easy as stencilling any other surface. Use good fabric paints, like Dylon Colourfun or Le Franc & Bourgeois, which can be 'fixed' by

pressing with a warm iron. With sheer fabrics like muslin, stretch the fabric over clean paper (old wallpaper for instance) so that you have a flat surface to stencil and the surface below is protected from excess paint passing through the sheer fabric.

Paint can do wonders for odd bits of junk furniture; here a Victorian whatnot has been given an exciting Crackle glaze finish, in white over pale blue, and a little Violet stencil has been casually dropped at each corner.

The Crab Apple Bathroom

The
Crab Apple Bathroom

This cluster of small rosy **crab apples** and leaves is the principal stencil element in this stencil set. This is a strong design with a lot of impact.

There are few prettier sights than a Crab Apple tree, either garlanded with spring blossom or studded with tiny vivid autumn fruit.

CRAB APPLE HARVEST or Fruit in Abundance

Chunky and colourful, the Crab Apple stencils build up an overall design quickly and effectively, completely transforming the Lloyd Loom chair in our photograph and dramatising a simple oval mirror. Colours chosen here echo the buff and terracotta used for the colourwashed dado.

An extra **pair of leaves** can be used to add movement and variety to the basic stencil, or extend it to fill a space.

Improving on nature, you can stencil **flowers** and fruit together, adding charm and delicacy by stencilling the pink and white blossom at appropriate points; or, like us, use a soft colour which tones with your room scheme.

1 Mix up a good green for leaves, adding a little white if the colour is too strong. Green is one of the most difficult colours to choose. A huge range exists but many of them have an unnatural and chemical brilliance. The green you use must complement both the fruit and the blossom, so take time to choose the perfect shade.

2 We used vermilion as our basic Crab Apple colour, but you might prefer yellow or crimson. Mix apple colour separately, using a clean brush, and stencil as for leaves, taking care to keep leaves and fruit separate.

RUSTIC ART

ADD A pretty posy of pink apple blossom to give a more feminine look to the basic stencil. Keep blossom colour related to the fruit, but much softer. Crab Apple blossom is usually a fresh pink and white, but we have used a warmer peachy pink to tone in. By repeating the fruit and flower motifs and adding extra leaves, you can rapidly build up a border, wreath, or overall pattern.

SUBTRACT It is very easy to extrapolate one small element from the main stencil for a particular purpose — simply choose a suitable decorative cluster of fruit or flowers from the main stencil and use on its own. Tiny stencils like these look pretty decorating furniture and accessories and help to carry the theme through.

3 Stencilled twigs now tie the design together. Use greenish brown for these, and at the same time you can stipple Crab Apples lightly with the same colour, to give a more solid effect.

4 The leaves can be enriched by stippling lightly with brown or with a paler green, made by adding a little white to the basic leaf colour. Stand back and look at your stencilled design, to check whether you like the shaded effect and colour balance before continuing. Superimposing colours like this gives a more subtle effect, and prevents the design looking hard.

ADAPT To create a diadem shape, which sits prettily above pictures, door frames, bedheads, etc., arrange stencil elements as shown, adding leaves and fruit as the space requires, and taking care to build up an expressive overall shape.

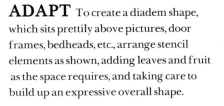

39

A bright profusion of Crab Apple stencils used in unexpected ways has given new interest and excitement to this very standard small bathroom. Basic colours here are off-white and buff Colourwash, with a band of terra-cotta at dado height. Wall colours have been chosen to complement jewel bright Crab Apples and green leaves.

AN ORCHARD ON TAP

Carrying a stencil theme through, as here, gives rooms an enviably integrated look — here even the towels have stencilled clusters of fruit.

Use strips of masking tape to mark out a tile pattern like this; the painted grid and stencilled border is a very effective way of visually upgrading an unexciting floor. We used the same colour to accentuate the vertical planks of the old-fashioned cottage door.

Dropping a cluster of stencilled fruit into the outer squares of the painted floor creates the look of an expensive tiled border, as well as adding welcome colour. It's fun to add little personalised details like the small cluster on the bathmat — almost anything can be stencilled. Here, one really splendid burst of stencil colour on a simple bathroom chair brings the whole scheme into focus, as well as transforming a very ordinary piece of furniture.

Stencilled clusters either side of the window, linked by a border stencilled on to a simple canvas blind, give a new definition to this corner of the room. Notice how the flamboyant colours in this mixed bunch of dried and natural flowers pick up the stencil tones on the wall behind. This is the sort of decorative trick or possibility which is made possible by introducing extra colour.

A RIPE CROP OF IDEAS

It's Attention to Detail that Makes the Difference

Stencilling is a truly compulsive activity, so be warned, you may not know when to stop! Each surface presents a new challenge and every texture will give a slightly different result. Experiment with colours and brushes until you find the effect you're happy with — if you stencil in a relaxed and confident way the pattern will flow and you will become absorbed in creative pleasure.

The contrast between flat wall surface and woven Lloyd Loom chair makes an attractive point. Stencilling on a textured surface like this is done in just the same way, but you may need to stipple the paint on more thickly, to build up colour in the crevices of the weave.

A very gentle, subtle effect, as here, is achieved with a slightly dampened brush, picking up a very sparing amount of colour. 'Wipe' the colour through the stencil with a circular motion. Build up colour variations by adding light touches of toning or contrasting colours.

Fabric painting is actually easier than wall painting. You work from above, so your arms feel more comfortable, and fabric absorbs paint, making blobs and bleeds less likely.

The matching Lloyd Loom linen basket is another natural for a stencilled uplift. Paint or spray the piece first, with two coats of paint (if using spray paints, work outside or with windows open for good ventilation). When base colour is quite dry, stencil as shown, not forgetting to protect your masterpiece with at least one coat of matt clear polyurethane varnish. Stencilling furniture like this is easy, and looks very attractive.

The Blackberry Bedroom

The Blackberry Bedroom

This graceful **spray of blackberries** is our main Blackberry stencil. It can be used in countless different ways, as shown in the ideas pages.

The twining growth of hedgerow blackberries, with their toothed leaves and clustering berries, provide an endlessly adaptable stencil subject. We show the separate stencil elements on this page.

GATHERING BLACKBERRIES

or Rich Pickings from a Country Lane

Used here as simple wreaths on plain unbleached calico bedcoverings and rambling naturalistically over the wall behind the bed, our Blackberry stencil has transformed the plainest of cottage bedrooms into a pretty and feminine bower. Following our clear step-by-step instructions for stencilling walls and fabrics will ensure that you too can achieve results as enchanting as these using the simplest materials.

A small extra **cluster of berries** can be combined with the main stencil, or used to create a small decorative flourish on its own.

Blackberry leaf spray can be used alone or combined with the berry cluster as shown overleaf.

Newly opened leaves for filling in spaces, and improving shape.

A friendly **caterpillar** to hide among the brambles for the children to find!

1 Mix a good green for the leaves and take some up on the brush. 'Stamp' the brush on a piece of waste paper to work off surplus colour. This will prevent any smudging. Fasten leaf stencil down with small tabs of masking tape, and stencil by brushing colour firmly through the cut-outs either with a dabbing motion or to and fro. Both give slightly different results.

2 Shading with a subtly toning colour over the plain green gives a livelier and more natural effect. Add a little brown to your basic leaf green for darker stippling, white and/or yellow for lighter leaves. Keep varying colours throughout for maximum effect.

THE ART OF NATURE

ADD elements of the stencil design to extend or develop the basic pattern. Never think of stencils as static tools — they can be used to give quite different effects by simply combining the elements differently. A small twiggy section added here begins to create the characteristic twining movement of wild blackberries, while extra leaves and berries can be added to extend the design.

SUBTRACT elements of the design for a simpler, more compact stencil. For some spaces — a box top, or a tray, perhaps — a smaller design is needed. It is perfectly easy to reduce the stencil size by dropping off end berries, as here, and leaving out the stalk and some of the leaves.

3 Now add berry clusters. Mix a blue/purple for ripe berries and stipple or brush them in as before. Mix a soft red for unripe berries and add these here and there for contrast. Take care not to overload your brush with wet colour, which can creep under the stencil and spoil the design.

4 Ripe berries need highlighting with a lighter stipple of white or pale mauve. This will soften them in line with the shaded leaf sprays. Check that you like the overall effect, remembering to stand back and look from across the room, as well as close up. This is the moment to adjust colours to please yourself and suit your room scheme.

INVERT It is surprising what a different look you get by simply turning a stencil over, and using it 'back to front'. Combining this reversed shape with the original ones helps to give the variety of growing natural things. Simply wash and dry the stencil before using it in reverse.

ADAPT Again, to build up a different shape, fill a particular space, or simply introduce more movement, stencil elements can be recombined in almost endless new arrangements. Never be afraid to experiment!

The simplest of elements combine to make an irresistibly pretty effect in this tiny cottage bedroom under the eaves. The airy sprays of our Blackberry stencil add charm and emphasis to traditional cottage features: tiny window, sloping walls and uneven plaster. Walls and ceiling were colourwashed in Plaster Pink, a muted greyish pink, making a gentle background for the twining Blackberry sprays in soft naturalistic colours.

BERRY DELICIOUS

Stencilled Blackberry wreaths dress up unbleached calico bedcoverings for a real designer effect. Carry the theme further with graceful rambling sprays over the bedhead, and outlining the window. Even the floor has a discreet Blackberry border. A design as airy and delicate as the Blackberry can be used intensely, as here, on almost every surface, but works equally well as a simple decorative border. The soft glowing colour and unassertive texture of colourwashed walls make an ideal background for informal floral stencils.

A little stencilling can have a lot of impact, as here, where a single spray draws attention to a traditional iron latch.

Anyone who has had to eradicate an unruly bramble bush from their garden will testify as to the plant's insidious invasive powers! This is one stencil design that cannot be overdone, so allow it to creep across all the surfaces in the room.

Half the fun of stencilling is finding new surfaces to decorate, and adapting different treatments to different situations. Here, the Blackberry design has been stencilled in a loose natural spray on the wall, counterpointed by a more formal border stencilled directly on to bare floorboards in non-naturalistic colours. More stencilled berries circling an upholstered chair seat in heavy cotton develop the theme still further. Naturalistic colours suit the cottage feel here, but the same design can be transformed by using unusual offbeat shades, or picking up an existing room colour.

FURTHER RAMBLINGS

It's Attention to Detail that Makes the Difference

Even experienced stencillers like to spend a little time putting a new design through its paces on rough paper. This familiarises you with the possibilities of the design in the way of positioning and recombining stencil elements, and often suggests quite new departures. Don't just play around with your stencil shapes — also experiment with different colourways and shading. These can be dramatically different, like, for instance, all-white berry sprays on a dark background, or they can simply be subtle tonal variations, as shown here, achieved by using different shading colours.

An occasional table in the same light oak as the cupboard is finished off with a loose wreath in the same muted shades-of-grey colour scheme. Seal table tops well with at least two coats of clear polyurethane varnish to protect your stencilled design.

Unbleached calico makes the prettiest cottage curtains, when bordered by our Blackberry stencils to match the arching clusters climbing up either side of this classic cottage window. Try a no-sew curtain solution by using iron-on hem bonding for all the seams. It has the added advantage of giving good, crisp edges.

A sturdy unpainted wooden cupboard gets the Blackberry treatment, using the leaf spray only, in off-white and grey for a subdued but decorative effect. Clusters of leaves are grouped on door panels and drawers, showing how using different colours changes the effect of the stencil. The final effect can be brightened or toned down by an application of tinted varnish. Use acrylic artists' paint to tint water-based varnish, and oil colours for traditional varnish.

Fabric stencilling opens up an exciting range of possibilities. Stencilling on fabric which will be seen close to, like a cushion cover, needs to be more precise than work on a larger scale. Fabric stencilling does not allow for second thoughts, so before venturing on to a square of expensive silk, practise on scrap material. For a complete contrast in texture, try stencilling on all sorts of surfaces, as here on a piece of packing case!

The
Anatolian
Living Room

The Anatolian Living Room

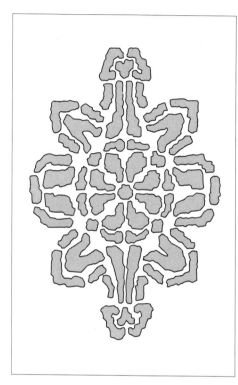

This bold **medallion motif**, with its echoes of tribal weaves, makes a strong design element in this stencil group, which can be used singly on a regular grid or combined with border stencils.

Some of the world's oldest patterns have been woven through centuries into rugs and hangings. They have a vitality which makes them look quite at home in contemporary settings.

STRONG COLOURS FROM THE STEPPES

or Turkish Delights from an Ancient Land

A chunky piece of Arts and Crafts furniture has been stripped and stencilled in strong clear colours.

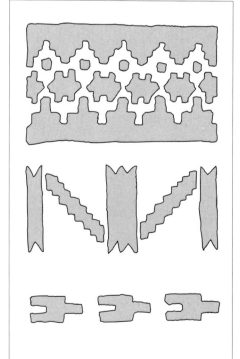

This **border stencil** has the rich colours and abstract shapes of so many kilims and flatweave rugs. Handsome on its own and exciting combined with the smaller borders.

Simply by varying the colours, this **geometric kilim motif** can be given a completely different appearance. It looks most effective used in one of the combinations shown on our stencilled wall hanging.

This **tiny border** looks almost absurdly simple, but stencilled in two contrasting colours, as shown on our chest, it makes a strikingly effective border.

1 This kilim-type border looks best in the strong but soft colours of vegetable dyes. Here a clear cobalt blue and orange red have been used. It is easier when stencilling in two colours on the same stencil to keep one brush for each colour. A small artist's brush is handy for stencilling in tiny details. Stencil bold patterns like these with a brushing movement for maximum texture, but make sure the brush is never overloaded with colour.

2 A great deal of the effectiveness of these traditional patterns comes from building them up in wide bands of pattern. This is how village women composed their beautiful rugs. Here the smallest border stencil is being added below the wide kilim border. It has been painted in the same cobalt blue.

A PILAF OF PATTERNS

ADAPT Do not be afraid to experiment with your Anatolian stencils as the tribal weavers always did. Simply using our zigzag border in reverse, you can create an attractive criss-cross motif which is strong enough to make an edge pattern.

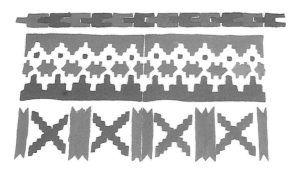

3 Moving the previous border along a notch, and stencilling between the previous shapes in contrasting red, gives a wonderfully compact and vigorous braided effect.

4 Still using the same colours, the third kilim border motif is stencilled just above the other two designs, showing what a rich effect can be produced with very simple motifs.

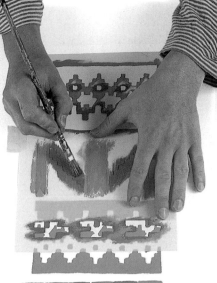

5 The medallion stencil also lends itself to a more complex colour treatment. This is not difficult but takes a little concentration to keep areas separate. Use a smaller artist's brush and fasten the stencil down with masking tape.

6 With the second colour and another small brush fill the remaining stencil areas as shown. Remember this is only one possible colour breakdown. Another painter might do it quite differently.

Who would imagine that a few metres of dyed hessian and some stencils could produce such a warm and luxurious effect? In the corner of this living room colours have been chosen from the 'Eastern Spices' range: saffron yellow and paprika orange for the two cushion covers.

GORGEOUS COLOURS AND RICH PATTERNS ADD UP TO EASTERN PROMISE

A build-up of glowing colour and strong patterns carries on the ethnic feel of kilim floor coverings and crewel work curtains, in this vivid and sunny sitting room.

AN EASTERN SPICE BAZAAR AT THE END OF YOUR PAINT BRUSH

It's Attention to Detail that Makes the Difference

The Anatolian stencil series can be used all over a house to add vibrant colour where it is needed. They are perfect designs to use for enlivening natural homespun textures/coarse hessian, scrubbed wood and rough textured wools. Choose earthy natural dye or spice colours, including white and black now and then. Any kilim rug or silk ikat weave will give you colour ideas. Stencilling can be rougher too: uneven colour touches of patchiness will just add to the 'hands on' effect.

A bold sweep of Anatolian pattern in sympathetic colours (white, blue and terracotta) is used to dramatise the simple iron grate and give the illusion of a deep skirting. Walls are painted a calm grey-green to offset so much brilliance and pattern everywhere else. You could key stencil colour to a natural rug. If in doubt stencil on paper strips to try the effect.

Using hessians in the wonderful colour range sold by Russell & Chapple in Covent Garden, and fabric paints by Le Franc & Bourgeois, produced this magnificent pile of exotic colour, which one could easily imagine transposed into a north African

Junkyards are still full of old pieces of furniture, which just need a thorough overhaul and some lively decorative touches to become the pride of your collection. Look for solid construction, simple shapes and hard woods if possible. Strip off old paint and varnish with commercial solvents. Dark open-grained woods (oak, ash) can be lightened by liming. After stencilling, protect all surfaces with matt clear polyurethane varnish (one or two coats).

hamman or, with a quick trip on the magic carpet, a Mongolian yurt (nomadic tent). These fabric paints can be used with a transparent medium, as for the dark stencil covers on our cushions, or with a colour lightener to give pale, opaque colours — e.g. our light blue over indigo.

A couple of metres of stencilled hessian in its natural biscuit colour makes a handsome wall hanging or patterned 'throw' to disguise an ugly chair. This rug-like effect was built up with all our Anatolian motifs. Colour lightener by Le Franc & Bourgeois was used as a white base for the remaining colours. Note especially the clever use of medallions and zigzag border for the centre panel.

The
African
Bedroom

This narrow **border** stencil is designed to be used either on its own or together with others in our African series.

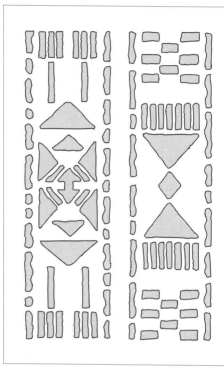

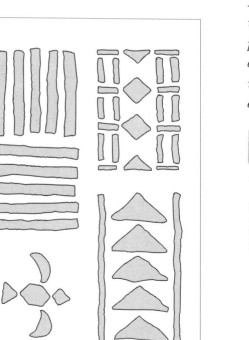

Although these vivid patterns have an almost abstract look, which makes them ideal for contemporary interiors, such as the delightful bedroom corner shown here, they are in fact ancient motifs which have been used by Nigerian weavers for centuries. Their bold geometric shapes suit simple furniture and understated rooms.

Lively **geometric shapes** look equally attractive interpreted in dark colours as in the bright shades used here.

AFRICAN BEDROOM
or Primitive Sophistication from Ancient Lands

Most of these motifs are linear since they were derived from hand weaves, but as the photographs in this book demonstrate they can be used in all sorts of different combinations to fill in spaces and add the emphasis of colour to your home.

This group of stencil **motifs** makes handy pattern 'blocks' to fill in larger spaces.

The stylised **bird** is our only naturalistic motif. Use it to highlight your stencilling. See opposite.

1 If you decide to use a range of colours like the ones shown here, you will find it easiest to stencil in one or two colours at one go, using a smaller separate brush for each colour and taking care not to confuse elements in the design. Here we have begun with blue and red for well-separated pattern elements.

2 This is where the fun begins. Using a vivid yellow and another small artist's brush, intervening parts of the stencil and a narrow border have been added. This immediately makes the design look 'more finished'.

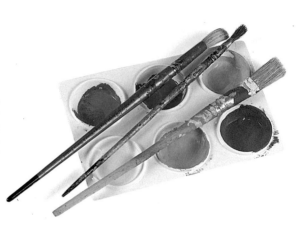

EXOTIC ART

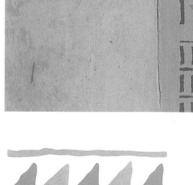

5 Another first step towards building up a two-colour border is shown here, using the same rich chalky blue. For a completely different look, this or any other of our African stencils would look great painted in indigo on white, or dark brown on a natural base colour.

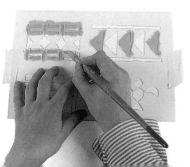

6 The previous design has been completed here with triangles and squares in brilliant yellow. It is entirely optional how these African stencils are divided by colour. It always helps to experiment first on paper with different possibilities.

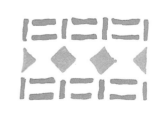

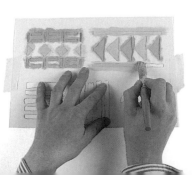

3 The same colour range is being used for this African stencil, but in a slightly different combination. The first step, as before, is to stencil in two out of the four colours used with brushes small enough to fill in fine detail in a controlled way.

4 Small details are now being filled in in blue with a separate brush, and the attractive border that results has something of the appeal of the traditional African bead works.

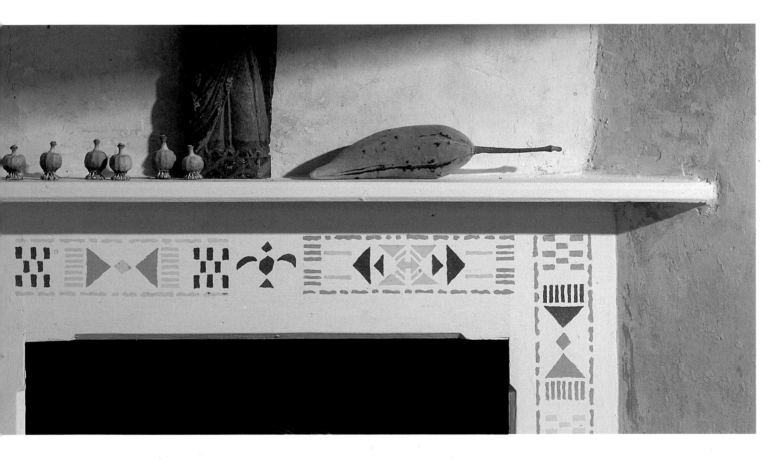

7 It is possible to get a great deal more mileage out of even the simplest stencils by turning them around and using them back to front, adding them together like tiles and mixing colour adventurously. Here the fourth in our African stencil series has been stencilled in a simple blue and yellow.

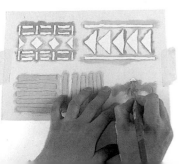

8 For a much more complex colour scheme the previous stencil has been used back to front here and with different colours, substituting red bars for the previous yellow. Overlaying red over yellow gives an interesting checked effect. This could be continued and repeated to make a very substantial border.

The various strip stencils in the African style have been combined here to make a colourful braid-like 'frame' for a small uncurtained window. The walls have been colour-washed in a neutral antique white finish, against which the vivid stencil colours show up handsomely. One of the pleasures of working with an informal-looking design like this one is that one does not have to aim for perfect symmetry; thus stencilling only goes round three sides of our window.

BRILLIANT LIGHT FROM THE DARK CONTINENT

Against a neutral colourwashing on walls, bright African textiles and stencil patterns sing out vibrantly. A little stencilling here goes a long way. It frames the odd-shaped windows and gives a touch of drama to a very plain little cottage fireplace surround.

IDEAS TO MAKE YOU GO NATIVE

It's Attention to Detail that Makes the Difference

Our African bedroom stencils are made to measure for decorating the simple chunky wooden pieces which look at home in country settings, and can still be found quite cheaply from junkyards, architectural salvage companies and street markets. The designs have a timeless quality which suits furniture of any period. Use strong colours and generous amounts of white for maximum contrast. A stencilled theme like this one does not have to be completed at one sitting. It makes sense and avoids backache and eye strain to add to it gradually.

This pile of gorgeously coloured African fabrics looks completely at home on top of the pine blanket box, which has been given an exciting new look with a simple stencilled border. Notice how the stencilled box fits in with the border on the wall behind, although quite different colours have been used.

Stencils show up well against the natural grain of stripped pine, but make sure you choose positive colours. More decoration could be added around the sides. An important thing to remember when stencilling on furniture is that all surfaces need to be protected with at least one coat of clear polyurethane varnish. On an old piece like this, matt or satin finish varnish gives a more sympathetic effect. Alternatively you could use a gloss varnish and then 'cut back' the shine with fine wire wool.

A very ordinary 50s-style wooden chair gets s new look with stencils used wittily to suggest a woven cane seat. Brick-red was used here and for the bird motif on the back. The other stencils on the back slat are done in off-white.

Another square window framed with stencilling gains enormously in visual interest. The carved bowl on the windowsill underlines the African feeling, while handwoven rugs and fabrics pick up our tribal colour scheme.

The
Indonesian
Bathroom

The Indonesian Bathroom

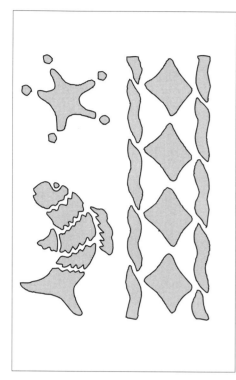

Inspired by the bright colours and decorative patterns of hand-printed Indonesian batik cottons, this attractive set of stencils has a marine theme, which is made to order for introducing eye-catching detail to your bathroom decor.

These can be **bubbles** floating round your batik fish, or simply a decorative flourish to add to your design where it needs build-up.

Whole shoals of **flying fish** can easily be suggested by repeating these vigorous designs. The different sizes help by introducing a touch of perspective — the smaller fish being the one further away.

Star fish?
Sea anemone?
This amusing stencil is just the kind of decorative shape that adds sparkle to an Indonesian border.

WONDERS OF THE DEEP

or a Colourful Catch from the Pacific Ocean

Some of the prettiest batik prints are based on just one colour, but gain texture and richness by combining several different shades in one design. Shades of blue look fresh and bathroomy, and add sophistication to a simple design.

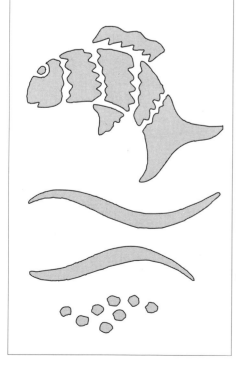

Most of our themed stencil sets contain at least one **border** design, because we find one straight horizontal element gives structure.

Stylised batik **waves** — add these to your Indonesian bathroom stencil design to suggest watery depths and give a flowing movement.

1 Start by mixing up two shades of blue, one dark and bright, and one pale and chalky, as here, to stencil the Indonesian border motif, or choose your own colour scheme to complement existing decor, bath tiles perhaps, or the colour of your bathroom suite. Stencil small details like the wavy border with a fine artists' brush, for neatness.

2 Switch to a fatter brush when stencilling in larger areas, like the casual diamond shapes which complete our Indonesian border stencil, because it will make the work go faster. The brush can either be used with a stippling action, for a light, even print, or brushed on in the conventional way for more texture.

OCEANIC ART

5 Pale blue waves combine with the starfish shape to create a properly fishy environment and a background for the leaping flying fish shapes.

6 The same fish stencil, but this time the fish is pointing down and has been stencilled on top of the wave motifs. This immediately gives a lively 'action' look to the design.

3 A leaping fish stencil added just above the border starts a decorative theme going, which could be repeated right round a bathroom, for a pretty frieze effect. We used the same darker blue for the fish.

4 A starfish shape in the paler blue balances the fish shape if you stencil it a bit below the border, as shown here, as well as adding a little flourish of its own to the overall design.

7 More waves and more fish — we have used the larger fish stencil, this time in the foreground — are used to build up quite a complex design with a lot of movement and a suggestion of space to it. A few bubbles add a finishing touch.

79

Walls and ceiling of this oddly shaped little bathroom are colourwashed in the same warm shade of terracotta, to give a feeling of unity, as well as a flattering background to the breezy blues and white chosen for the Patterns of the World Indonesian bathroom stencil.

WATER, WATER EVERYWHERE

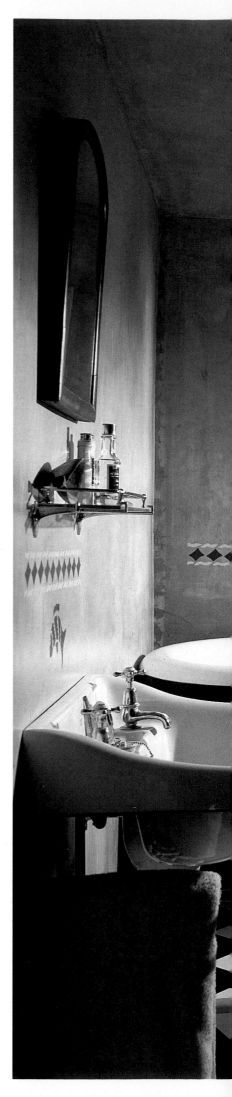

Half the fun of stencilling is using designs to link different elements in a room. This can give a really classy, personalised look to an interior. Don't forget that fabrics take kindly to stencilled flourishes. Stencils on bathroom furniture must be sealed with one or two coats of polyurethane varnish, preferably stencil gloss.

Cheaper than etched glass and just as pretty — a whole family of Indonesian stencils has been stippled in plain white on to clear glass. The border design looks a bit like a row of small tiles used as a decorative accent each side of the window. If you want stencilling on glass to be transparent, use special glass paints.

MARINE IDEAS FOR DRY LAND

It's Attention to Detail that Makes the Difference

There are so many things, even in a small, plainly furnished bathroom, which can be given a completely different look with a lick of paint and/or a few stencilled elements from our Indonesian Bathroom set. The simplest ideas are often the most effective, decoratively. Keep to a few colours and have fun with the expressive leaping fish shapes.

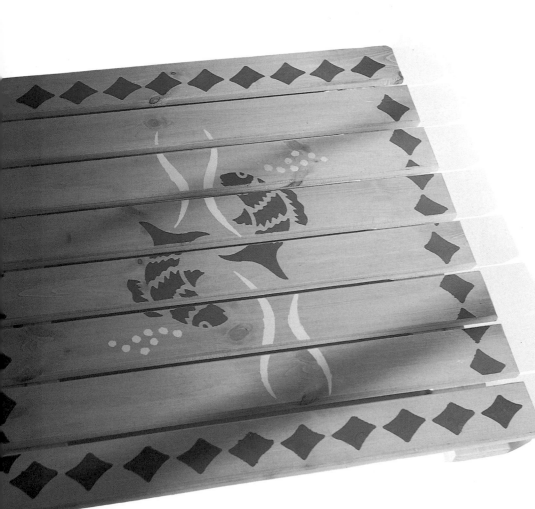

A slatted wooden bath platform has been colourwashed to match bathroom walls, and then decorated with a couple of leaping fish, border and bubbles, then varnished.

The sort of junk stool which you can still pick up quite cheaply looks dressed up enough to move into a drawing room by the time it has been nicely painted (we chose a pale cream eggshell), stencilled attractively in two shades of blue on top, and finished with a coat or two of clear matt or eggshell polyurethane varnish, to protect the decoration from wear and tear and steamy bathroom conditions.

One last fling with the Indonesian flying fish on the corner of a ribbed bathroom mat. Bath sets tend to be boringly plain: a quick pass with the stencil brush gives new interest. On heavily textured fabrics like this, the technique is the same, except that one needs to use more pressure on the brush with Le Franc & Bourgeois fabric paints.

The
Indian Kitchen

Themed stencils need a strong **border motif**, like this one, to give definition to a room scheme and balance other design elements.

The lacy 'gul' or **stylised leaf**, with its characteristic little twist, is one of the irresistible patterns of the world and is a natural for stencilling.

A small stencil motif like this is useful as a **'filler'** or for 'powdering' backgrounds - i.e. repeating a motif on a regular grid.

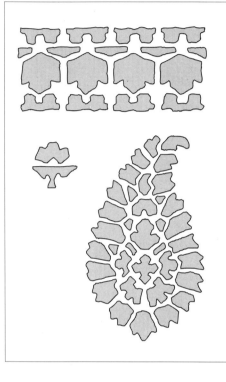

The textile crafts of India have created some of the great patterns of all time, subtle, timeless and stunningly decorative.

INDIAN IMPORTS

or How to Add Spice without Burning Yourself

Give your home the glamour and colour of hand-blocked Indian prints with the co-ordinated stencils in our Indian kitchen set. Used singly, or together, they build a rich filigree of pattern which can transform a room, furniture, textiles.

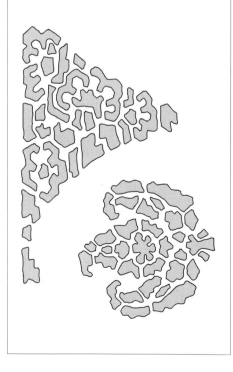

Arcading is the word for the pretty arched effect created by this stencil. Use the leaf or bird in the spaces.

A variant of **the classic 'gul' motif**, this stencil has a shape which vaguely suggests an exotically feathered bird.

1 Deep crimson has been chosen as the dominant colour in this stencil sequence. Use a medium artists' brush to stencil in main outlines, as here, but do not worry too much about colour 'straying'. The next stage will sort this out.

2 The missing bits of the border and 'gul' have been filled in with a deep blue for a colour combination with subtle impact. Choose your own colours to blend or contrast with existing decoration.

THE ART OF THE SPICE

4 Blue is the predominant colour used to stencil arcading and 'bind' motif, for a regularly repeating border, but contrast accents have been dotted in using orange and magenta (very Indian colours) and a fine brush.

5 To create an 'arcading' effect, simply tag the start of one stencilled motif on to the end of the previous one, as shown here, using the little extra 'bit' as a guide and making sure the horizontal edge is straight.

3 A characteristic Indian border design is beginning to come together. The second 'gul' is positioned parallel to the first, using the border edge as a guide line, and for variety its centre is stencilled in a pale violet. Over a large area small variations like this add great subtlety.

6 A majestic and exotic border results when the border stencil is used to define the upper limit, as here, using the same colours as before. The little 'sprig' motif added in magenta pink below the arcade gives the finishing touch.

All our Indian kitchen stencils bar one have been 'stacked up' to create the really magnificent border shown here stencilled in four colours — blue, yellow, magenta and scarlet. Because Indian motifs are lacy rather than solid, bright colours can be used without risk of the end result looking garish, but try to go for a balanced mix, as here, where top border colours echo colours of the 'gul' frieze below, and contrast with predominantly blue 'arcading'.

HOME FROM THE TRADE ROUTES

The 'full dress' border focuses attention on the two most important features of this pleasant traditional-looking kitchen, the window seat and the splendid cream enamelled Aga, but details — mats, dish towels — pick up and reinforce our Indian theme.

Stone walls and simple, sturdy furniture create an unassertive context where the dramatic colours and flowing shapes of our Indian kitchen stencils have real visual impact. Accessories are a natural place for these gorgeous patterns, and napkins and dish cloths are only two of the kitchen textiles you can transform, adding instant glamour and interest to daily chores.

TASTY IDEAS FROM EASTERN LANDS

It's Attention to Detail that Makes the Difference

The border stencil used on its own makes a bold band of colour and pattern behind a worktop. This stencil would also look good as a bolder surround to a painted floor, because the shapes are strong enough to 'read' clearly. The centre space might then be filled in with a 'powdering' of leaf shapes stencilled on a regular grid, as for a printed cotton.

A couple of hours' stencilling can make your table arrangements memorably colourful and cheer up the simplest meal. Cork table mats, linen and paper napkins are all ideal for stencilling, and here we show some ways to arrange motifs for different shapes.

The
Tulip
Parlour

The Tulip Parlour

The tulip stencil is rich enough to be used on its own as in the frieze opposite, or it can be combined with other pattern elements for a stunning effect.

William Morris designed the flamboyant tulip motif in this set of Gothic-inspired stencils for a Victorian Gothic house, Stanmore Hall. It was one of the last commissions Morris undertook.

STANMORE TULIPS

or Flowers from a Morris Garden

The heraldic character and decorations of Morris's splendid tulip do not look out of place stencilled in rich creams and reds in a modest front parlour.

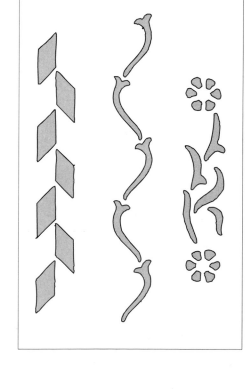

This slender **wavy border** stencil makes a useful 'filler' when building up a pattern.

Another small **border motif** from Stanmore Hall that is decorative enough to use on its own.

In a rather different mood this bold **chevron** design makes a striking narrow border, as shown in the picture opposite.

Dramatically simple borders like the chevron can be just as decorative as more elaborate ones. Use it for outlining walls, windows, doors etc, like a decorative braid. In Stanmore Hall, the chevron was used in two colours as detail on the magnificently painted staircase. The Morris chevron uses alternating black and white, which gives an almost rope-like solidity, but it looks just as strong stencilled, as here, in one colour.

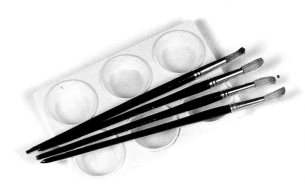

BLOOMING ART

1 Formal yet lively, our Morris tulip stencil has something medieval about it. It could have been inspired by a rare Ottoman embroidery. It makes a strong pattern 'block' painted in one colour, as here, or in the tone-on-tone frieze shown in our main picture, where the stencil colour is matched to woodwork.

2 The frieze is continued by simply lining up tulip stencils and repeating the process. Busy designs like this with many cut-outs should be fixed in place with masking tape tabs. Use a medium-sized brush. Again take care not to overload the brush with paint, smudging the fine stems and leaves.

The wavy border needs to be painted with a rather finer brush, taking care not to overload it with paint because the delicacy of a design like this would be spoiled by careless smudging. Use tabs of mashing tape to hold the stencil down while working.

Considering the simplicity of its elements, this little floral border is brilliantly effective, typical of Morris in its combination of stylised pattern-making with naturalistic movement. It has something of the look of old embroidery and could be stencilled in two colours rather than the plain red used here.

3 Two of the small borders are combined with the tulip motif to create a frieze with the richness of Morris's original decoration at Stanmore Hall. If more colours were used the effect would be as rich as a typical William Morris design or one of his beautiful linen-union fabrics.

William Morris's medieval soul would surely have delighted in
the stirring heraldic colouring of this small but distinctive
front parlour, with its typical tiled fireplace and gilded overmantel
mirror. Fireplace and ceiling have been left white for contrast,
otherwise the crimson theme predominates.

THE WARMTH OF THE PARLOUR

People are often nervous of using strong colours in room decoration.
Our photograph shows how easily a strong colour theme, like the
matching crimson on upholstery, walls and curtains, can be
lightened by a clever use of contrasting patterns and fabrics. The
Morris frieze on the walls adds richness. The same designs
stencilled on to simple checked and striped fabric look lively,
modern and add freshness to the overall colour scheme.

The Morris tulip motif back-to-back makes an excellent shape for decorating a square surface. Here two bright cushions' deep maroon fabric paint contrasts well with the red and white check.

The attractive rush-seated settle based on a traditional Sussex design is a Morris original. All our Morris tulip parlour stencils are combined here to dramatise a Victorian bay window, often a difficult feature to decorate. Chevrons frame the bay, repeated tulip motifs draw attention to side walls, while tulips and borders together make a handsome frieze just above the red-painted skirting.

It only takes quarter of an hour to transform completely a small item of furniture like this useful ordinary side table. Stencilling in subdued pale maroon, using back-to-back tulips and a border, is enough to dress up a dark stained finish and give an effect almost like marquetry. Stencilling can be very effective done on unpainted wood. Try tinting varnish with raw umber for an antique look which will give added protection. Remember to use oil colour with traditional varnish and acrylic colour with a water-based varnish.

A close-up shows how effectively tulip stencils can be combined to make the sort of framed 'panel' which Morris himself often used in his interiors. The tulip motif itself is ideal for dramatising blank spaces. Three repeats framed by the chevron are enough to give a finished look.

INSPIRED BY STANMORE

It's Attention to Detail that Makes the Difference

The characteristic colours we have used for the sumptuous tulip parlour scheme were inspired by one of the hand-printed colourways used for the William Morris design shown here. Tone-on-tone stencilling like this is a subtle way of using elaborate motifs, adding texture and richness without being oppressively busy.

Rush-seated settle, chairs and knot-rug and the complete William Morris archive may be viewed at the William Morris Gallery, Lloyd Park, Forest Road, London E17

The
Willow
Study

The
Willow
Study

Without being over-elaborate the **Willow stencils** fill their allotted space handsomely. Use this stencil together with the one below.

It would be hard to think of a motif more typical of Morris's robust Englishness than the willow design he created for the London home, 1 Palace Green, of the Earl and Countess of Carlisle.

THE NOBLE WILLOW

or Leafy Boughs from a Riverbank

A pattern as fresh and vigorous as our Morris Willow stencil needs to stand alone as a decoration, with nothing more complicated than a simple stylised rope border to act as a 'frame'. Here it is decoratively highlighting prized possessions above a painted Victorian fireplace.

A chunky **small border** can be used on its own, or can be 'doubled up' as shown, by using two colours and stencilling over gaps. This works better as a framing device.

This is the **Willow stencil** to use on its own as a decorative block, because there are no loose ends and the design is compact.

For a strong rope effect, choose two contrasting colours for stencilling. A simple chunky stencil like this can be stencilled quite fast using a fat artists' brush, and either a stippling or standard to-and-fro technique. Stick stencils down with tabs of masking tape.

The rope stencil has been moved along a space, filling in gaps in the previously stencilled section. Use masking tape to hold the stencil in place, when necessary, and always pick up the minimum colour on your brush to avoid smudging.

RIVERSIDE ART

2 The second Willow stencil section fits on to the end of the first one to make a continuous flowing design, as shown here. To elongate as a border, simply repeat this process, stencil one, then two, right across the wall.

3 The Willow section shown in the previous picture is being doubled up here, with one length of pattern directly beneath the first, to make a rich 'panel' of decoration. This was a decorative device Morris often used himself, both for stencil schemes and as book ornaments for the beautiful books he designed for the Kelmscott Press.

1 The Willow stencil really needs to be taped down, because it is a more elaborate design which takes a few minutes to paint. Use a medium artists' brush and stipple fine stems, for a precise outline. Start at one side and stencil across, taking care not to overload your brush.

4 The rope pattern has been used here to frame the panel of stencilled willow leaves. Conventionally, framing designs are mitred at the corners for a neatly squared off look, but as our photo shows, leaving the ends 'free' looks good too, and saves a lot of time.

Morris and Co. used stencils like wallpaper, covering entire walls and ceilings too with bands of design — often half a dozen different designs to a room—executed in different colours for an opulent, glowing polychrome effect which was the height of fashion in the late 19th century.

A STUDY OF LEAF & BOUGH

A simplified version of the Morris approach shows how spectacular a solid panel of stencilled 'Willow' looks in a small study/bedroom, adding interest and drama to the cream-painted wall behind a sofa bed outlined with the same rope stencilling. More rope stencil is shown in the detail shot.

The idea of breaking up painted surfaces, with applied decoration, to form 'panels' is as old as Pompeii. A similar approach was fashionable in Gustavian-style rooms in late 18th-century Sweden. What this very simple visual illusion does is give blank, boring surfaces a suggestion of architectural structure. Panels outlined with a rope, stencilled as shown here, can help to give coherence to a lot of unrelated objects or to 'frame' prized possessions, like the two modern prints and the elegant model boat.

A designer of endless invention himself, William Morris would almost certainly have enjoyed thinking of new uses for, and combinations of, stencilling motifs. Morris and Co. frequently stencilled furniture as well as walls and ceilings, usually as a surround for larger painted panels.

WILLOW TIPS

It's Attention to Detail that Makes the Difference

The two Morris-inspired stencil designs in our Willow set can be used to dramatise a contemporary room and simple furniture, as our pictures here demonstrate. Do not imagine that stencilling has to be very intense to look effective. Sometimes an idea that takes only minutes can make all the difference.

One nice thing about a strong pattern element in a room scheme is that it can become a focus for more bright colours and strong designs. The pile of colourful cushions and the richly striped silk throw on our painted day-bed are a case in point.

A spray or two from the Morris Willow stencil makes a pretty decorative detail for the head of the painted day-bed. Maximising stencils in this way is the mark of a good stenciller, and finding new uses for a design is rewarding and fun.

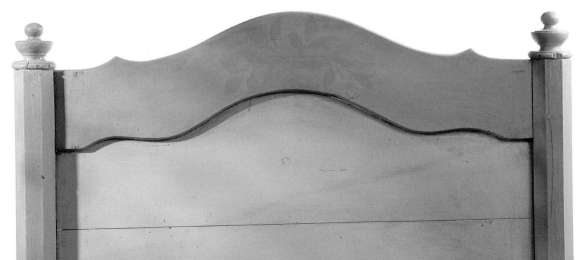

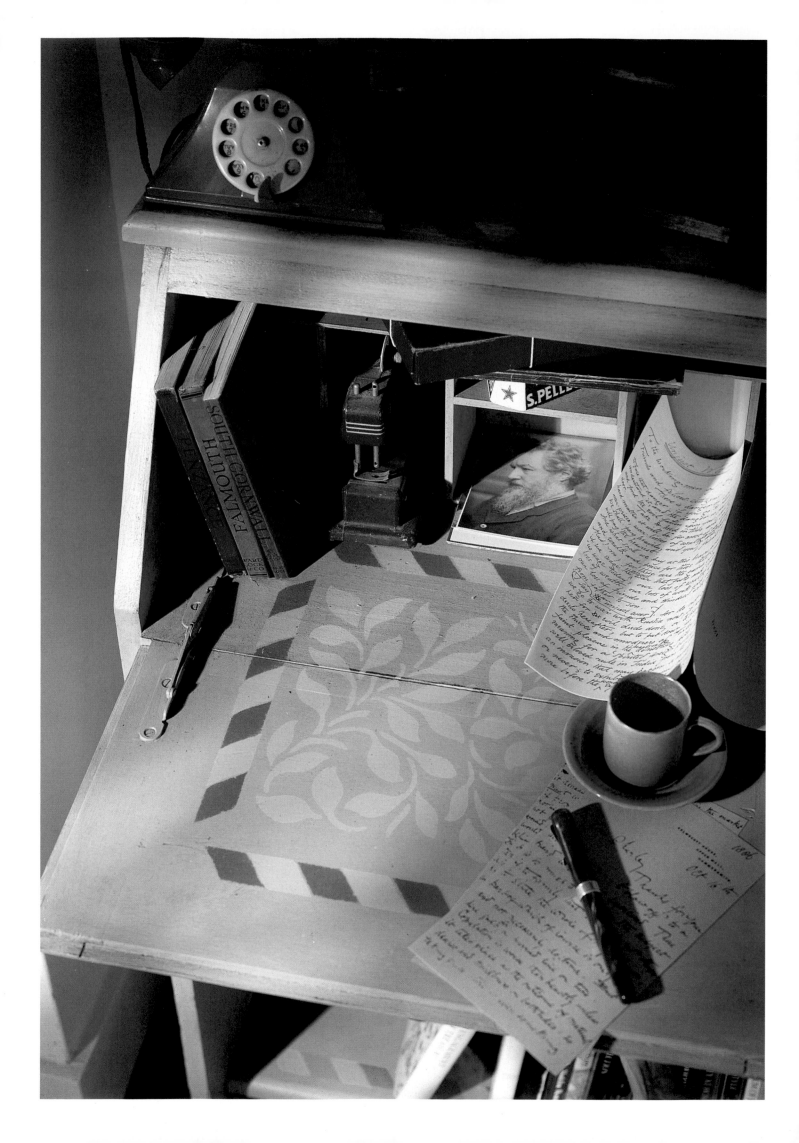

The
Daisy
Bedroom

The Daisy Bedroom

Daisy, designed in 1864, is one of Morris's first three wallpaper designs. Like all his first work, it looks as fresh today as it did over a century ago. The stylised daisy shapes have a medieval air, a charming symmetry which recalls illustrations in old herbals, as well as the flowery meadows of medieval tapestries and illuminated manuscripts.

Different in detail, but alike in their daisy freshness, these two stencils give the basic **flower and leaf shapes** used in Morris's wallpaper, as well as his own original colourway. Another quite different, but successful, colourway combines red flowers and green leaves on a white ground.

DESIGNER DAISIES

or Fragrant Posies of the Arts & Crafts

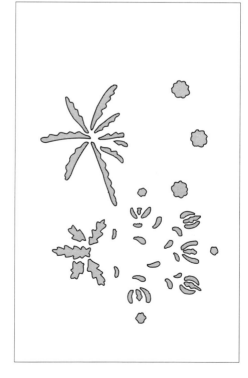

Morris's own Daisy wallpaper played up the formality of his subtly contrasting daisy motifs by repeating them on a grid, in the medieval decorative technique called 'powdering'. Stencilling allows you to play with variations on this theme, as shown opposite, where opening a cupboard door reveals an unexpected and delightful flowerbed.

These stencils, painted over the basic shapes, add contrasting details — **flower centres, leaf veins**. The deliberate stylisation and use of a strong contrast colour emphasise the 'old embroidery' look Morris was aiming for.

1 Part of the fun and versatility of stencils lies in experimenting with different colour combinations to find which suits your decorating scheme best. A vibrant yellow, as here, gives a completely different effect to more conventional pink and white. Use masking tape to hold the stencil in place and a medium artists' brush to colour in flowers with a stipple action.

FLOWERING ART

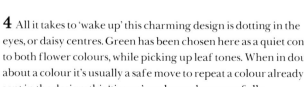

4 All it takes to 'wake up' this charming design is dotting in the eyes, or daisy centres. Green has been chosen here as a quiet contrast to both flower colours, while picking up leaf tones. When in doubt about a colour it's usually a safe move to repeat a colour already present in the design: this 'ties up' a colour scheme usefully.

2 Using a second brush and a different colour, stencil in a second group of daisies, here shown in a non-naturalistic but pretty sky blue. To expand this motif into a border simply repeat it as shown, lining up the base of the stencil each time. Some people like to complete each section, others tackle stencilling one colour at a time.

3 A rich mid-green is stippled or 'powdered' to make the expressive leaf and stem patterns. Use a medium artists' brush and take up colour very sparingly on the bristles to produce a crisp, clear image. Fine detail like this requires greater precision and control in stencilling — smudging shows up more! Test brush first on newspaper.

5 The final finish to the bright eyed daisy goes on in a neat black shade (mix black and raw umber with leaf green) used to stipple sharp detailing on leaves and stacks. When using several colours on one stencil, as here, it makes sense to stock up on brushes — one to each colour, to save time and possible confusion.

*No need, as this picture shows, to feel bound by the
Master's precedent. The neat and tidy effect of
Morris's daisy motifs is underlined wittily in this cool
painted bedroom by taking a daisy border round
the walls at dado height, like an embroidered girdle,
and massing a whole regiment of daisies in a
colourful 'block' above the fireplace.*

A DAISY GARLAND CAST AROUND

A rather ordinary wardrobe looks unrecognisably pretty given a two-tone (same blue as the walls plus a very pale blue for panels) paint finish and ten minutes' attention with daisy stencils. No need to smother a painted piece with decoration — less is often more with stencils.

William Morris's design skills are to be marvelled at. Each leaf, stem, stalk and flower shape, taken in isolation, is perfectly proportioned in both naturalistic and design terms. He manages to capture the essence of the plant's energy and then keeps it flowing through the static designs.

IDEAS FROM THE MEADOWLAND
It's Attention to Detail that Makes the Difference

It is a fact, and yet a mystery, that a Morris design is immediately recognisable without being at all eccentric or manoeuvred. Another mystery, which has been baffling other designers ever since, is how it is that a Morris design can be over a hundred years old, familiar as one's own signature, and yet come up year after year as fresh as the proverbial daisy. Here we demonstrate the versatility of a successful motif, adding blithe springtime freshness to the walls, woodwork and furniture of our simple Daisy Bedroom.

Who needs pictures when a painted patch of daisies looks so superbly decorative? The clear, pretty colours used here are Morris's own first choice, yellow and white adding sunshiny warmth to plainly painted sky blue walls. Note how daisies are 'staggered' from one row to the next, for visual interest.

It doesn't take ten minutes to lavish stencilled daisies on a plain panelled door, but that is the nature of a 'finishing touch' which can make all the difference to a room, make it feel cherished, like a beautifully wrapped parcel. The daisy motif is a natural for brightening simple shapes and plain surfaces.

A nicely balanced trio of daisies, stencilled in the top panel of a cupboard door, gives an attractive sophisticated look to an undistinguished painted piece. Juggle patterns around to find new combinations and space fillings, when stencilling.

The rusticity of a stripped pine blanket box is charmingly complemented by a stencilled 'meadow' on top. Colour schemes need not be elaborate to score. Plain white daisies and dark green leaves could not be simpler or more decorative against warm-toned wood, but remember to give a protective coat of clear polyurethane varnish over stencils.

The

Brother Rabbit Kitchen

The
Brother Rabbit
Kitchen

A pair of song thrushes in a maze of foliage creates an almost heraldic effect in this splendidly decorative stencil from the Brother Rabbit set, which can be used on its own or in various combinations, as shown.

With its exuberant yet controlled plant forms enclosing lively pairs of birds and rabbits, this Brother Rabbit design was intended as a fabric print, and shows William Morris's genius for enlivening large formalised patterns with freshly observed naturalistic detail.

FAUNA IN HIDING

or Pretty Camouflage at Home

The rich complexity of 'Brother Rabbit' allows it to be separated into three key motifs for stencilling, without loss of vitality. Morris intended to use simple colour schemes for elaborate patterns, so just two colours, blue and green, have been used throughout the Brother Rabbit kitchen, letting the interest and flow of the design speak for itself.

A stylised **'pomegranate'** shape made up of oak leaves and acorns casts interesting light on Morris's use of exotic motifs, re-worked to give them a flavour at once very English, and very William Morris.

The **Brother Rabbits** themselves are shown crouched under waving dock leaves for a dramatic stencil, strong enough to stand alone as a border motif.

126

1 This is a 'busy' stencil though it is being interpreted very simply, using dark blue for bird and rabbits to make them stand out against green stems and foliage. This design requires some formality, so measure and plan the area to be filled before you begin stencilling.

2 Birds have been carefully stencilled in blue, with a firm artists' brush, in the spaces, and one or two leaves elsewhere have been coloured blue too, to create a secondary rhythm in the design, which might otherwise look 'spotty' and restless.

UNDERGROWTH ART

5 Almost as complex as the Morris original, the bird and pomegranate shape is now being underpinned by two sets of rabbit stencils, to make a dense block of pattern which could be used on a bed head, chair back or seat. Keep colours simple for maximum effect: Brother Rabbit looks stunning in all red or off-white, for instance.

3 The pomegranate is designed to slot in neatly between bird stencils and make up a continuous border. Here the pomegranate has been added in green predominantly, with touches of dark blue.

4 This shows how handsomely the Brother Rabbit stencil design grows through simple repetition. A shape like this would look very decorative filling a narrow horizontal surface — drawer front, box lid, door panel.

ADAPT With a bit of juggling stencils can be arranged to fit around a simple grate and mantelpiece in the Brother Rabbit kitchen. Bird and pomegranates strung together make pendants either side, and a row of pomegranates (minus stalk) makes a pretty row of 'tiles' along the top.

129

A humble back kitchen in a suburban cottage simply doesn't recognise itself, thanks to the lavish use of Brother Rabbit stencils on just about every surface in sight, including the painted and varnished floor. Remember that complex-looking stencils with dozens of cut-outs are no more difficult to use than simpler-looking ones, they just take a little longer to complete.

Uniform paint colour and stencils give a co-ordinated look to a quite random collection of useful junk pieces — a handy trick when furnishing a kitchen on the cheap.

SISTER BIRD, BROTHER RABBIT

Indefatigably creative, a man of immense energy and enthusiasm, William Morris achieved a rare fusion in his design work, of robust strength and an almost feminine delicacy and sensitivity. It is the tension between the two aspects of his nature that gives a Morris design panel such inexhaustible vitality.

Just for fun, and to make a visual link with the kitchen, quaint wooden stairs acquire a painted 'carpet', patterned (like the skirting) with pomegranates, light on dark for a change.

KITCHEN CLEVERNESS

It's Attention to Detail that Makes the Difference

Tongue-and-groove was never like this. Dark blue-green paint on the plank walls creates striking vertical lines if the intervals are left white, and picks up the idea already stated by the painted floorboards and stair 'carpet'. Brother Rabbit stencils have enough impact to stand up to a bold decorating scheme like this one, adding contrast and movement where needed, as well as underlining architectural features as only stencils can.

Rescued from a skip and given a paint and stencil treatment, a sturdy stool takes an honourable place in the Brother Rabbit kitchen. Morris preferred simple traditional shapes in furniture, and they are the best choice for our stencils.

Somewhere between bench and pew, this seat has the simple shape and plain surfaces that are particularly successful as a background to intricate, lacy stencils like these. For a softer effect, a length of natural cotton or canvas could be stencilled to match and make up into a seat cushion. Use special fabric paints, washable if sealed with a warm iron.

Another example of the sort of junk item to look out for. Our photo shows how attractive a bedside cabinet (doubling as a vegetable rack) can look with a lick of new paint and some well located stencils. If painting straight lines defeats you, cheat with two lengths of masking tape stuck down a line's breadth apart. Varnish over stencilled furniture to protect it, especially in a kitchen.

The
Tartan
Dining Room

The
Tartan Dining Room

To launch the Scottish theme of our Tartan dining room stencils, a little stylised **thistle** to work in with other motifs together with a streamlined **flag**.

The key stencil in this set, a block of **Tartan weaves**, can be extended in all directions to create a bold openwork design.

There is a contemporary feel to plaids and tartans which make them a perfect choice for stencilling colour on to a plain modern interior.

HIGHLAND FLING

or Tartan for the Style of Today

Tartan patterns are among the oldest known, the result of combining different coloured threads in a continuously woven fabric. Scotland is famous as the home of the clan tartan, but plaid fabrics have been made in countries as far apart as Ireland and India, and their colourful simplicity never palls.

A small **'fleur de lys'** motif, which could be part of a Cairngorm highland dress pin, makes a neat stencil motif.

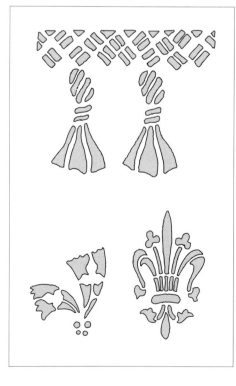

Braid and tassels like these cost a mint made up of real threads, but you can get the same effect with paint and stencils for mere pennies.

As a variant on a tassel theme but with a more Scottish flavour, these little **tags** can be added to our design elements.

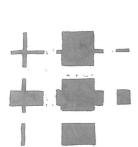

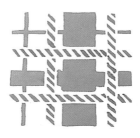

1 Using a strong green and a medium-sized artists' brush, stencil the main solid areas of the Tartan grid stencil. A straight-edged stencil like this needs crisp definition. To achieve this, take care not to overload your brush and use a stippling movement to paint in finer detail.

2 Using a different colour — we chose a sparkling turquoise blue— and a finer brush, paint in the striped threads that make up our magnified Tartan grid design. Of course you can substitute your own colours for these.

THE SCOTTISH ART

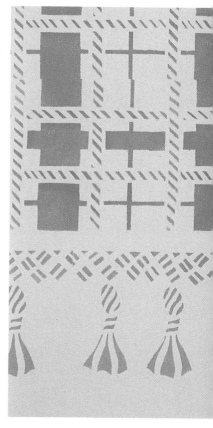

4 It is a peculiarity of our Tartan grid that it can be used any way up. Here the previous band of stencilling is shown up-ended, while a band of braid and tassels is added at the bottom. Multiplied, this combination gives the splendid frieze shown overleaf.

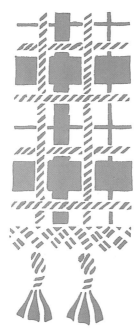

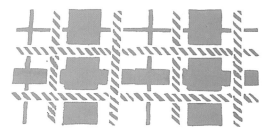

3 To start building up a really impressive length of Tartan for a frieze or a border, repeat the previous stencilling sequence, lining up the central solid stripes. If you are stencilling up close to the ceiling, pencil a line round the walls to act as a guide and keep your Tartan travelling in a straight line.

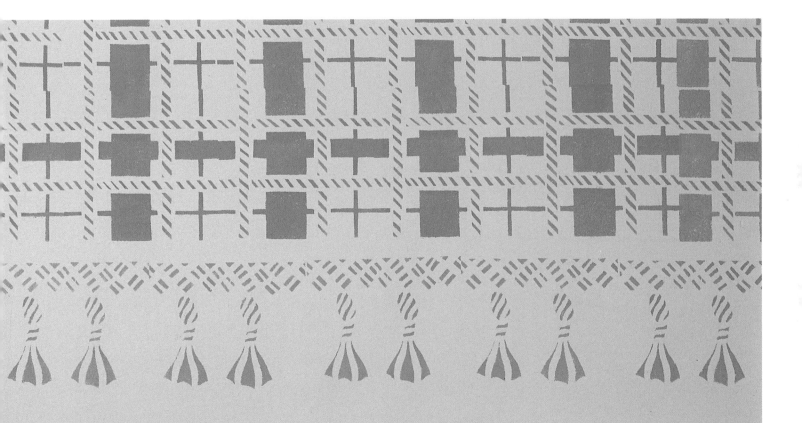

5 To make a continuous braid and tassels border, pencil a horizontal line as a guide and keep repeating the motif shown, overlapping the braid sections a little each time.

ANY ONE of these small motifs repeated on a grid would make a lively and attractive design for fabrics, furniture and other services. Use a fine brush and take care not to pick up too much colour, because small motifs need a precise touch.

This cool and elegant dining room has been painted in a soft sky-blue and hunting Stewart green, with plenty of pale contrasting fabric and paintwork to freshen and lighten the overall effect.

I'LL BE IN SCOTLAND BEFORE YE

Using the dark green over the ceiling seems to lower the room's apparent height. The stunning use of our Tartan stencil as a deep tasselled frieze adds interest where it is needed, helping to bridge the gap between dark and pale colours. Note that the ceiling green has been repeated in the Tartan. More stencils enliven simple creamy canvas fabrics on the furniture and cushions.

The most ordinary wooden folding chair goes upmarket if you decorate it with a few simple stencil designs. Choose a pale colour for contrast. Do not worry too much about getting everything exactly symmetrical — a little variation looks lively. Varnish with clear matt polyurethane to protect it.

A long shot of the green wall 'powdered' with our highland motifs makes an attractive background to large china vases.

ARTFUL IDEAS WITH TARTAN

It's Attention to Detail that Makes the Difference

It is quick and fun to stencil small motifs on room accessories like the ones shown here, but it can make a lot of difference to a room scheme, introducing a little colour and interest and giving a 'throughout' look. Sticking to the same colours throughout is a way of guaranteeing that it all hangs together in the final result.

A close-up picture shows how dramatically a small motif can lift a dark background colour, like our hunting Stewart green. Stencilled surfaces look happy together, as the chair indicates.

Cushion covers as simple as pillow cases are fashionable and easy to make. Use a fine-sheeting grid cotton, or a pastel chintz. A few hand-stencilled motifs give them a luxury look. If you find sewing too daunting, then choose from the many plain-coloured, ready-made cushion covers on the market. Simply slip a sheet of card inside to prevent the colour from seeping through, and stencil it with your chosen motifs.

More plain cream cotton dramatised by our Tartan stencil collection makes a very classy table cover, matched overleaf by a simple chair cover.

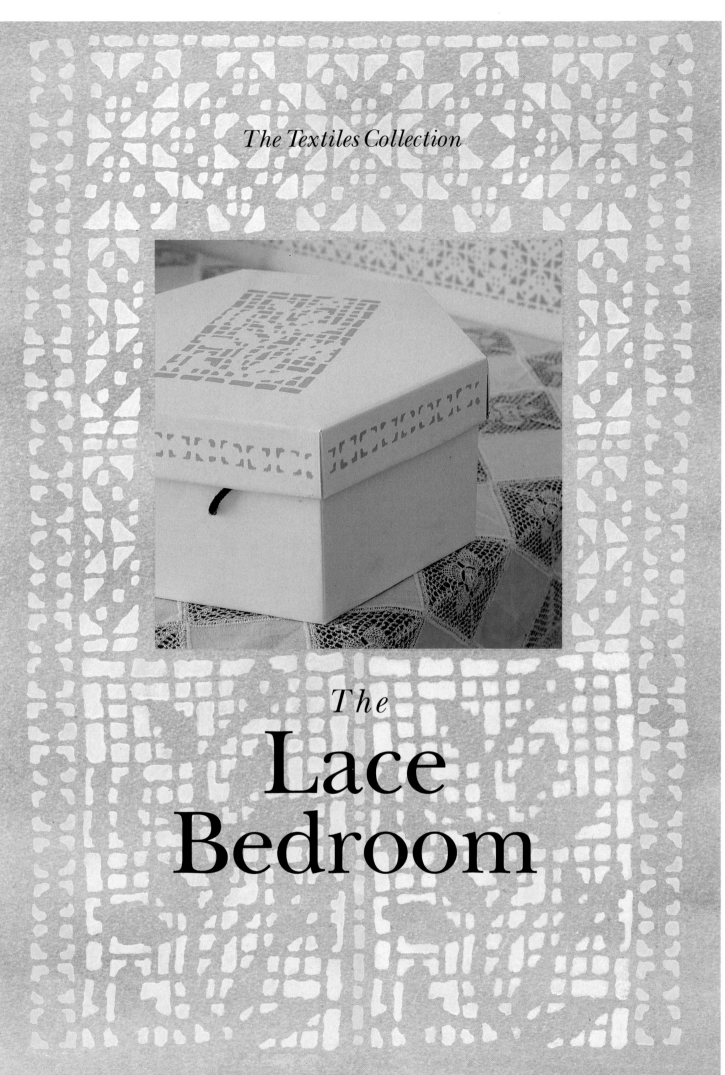

The Lace Bedroom

The Lace Bedroom

A wide border with a **geometric motif** to use on its own, girdling the walls, or together with our other Lace stencils to make panels.

It really doesn't take long to stencil this narrow **lacy border-like trimming** round bedroom walls, doors and windows. It is meant to meander slightly — this is a relaxed stencil set.

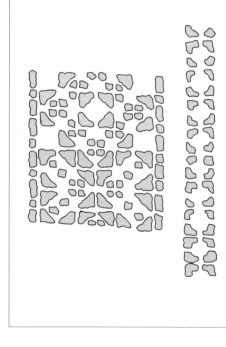

Nothing could be more decorative than the airy openwork motifs of old-fashioned hand-crocheted lace, which we have translated into stencils.

DOING UP LACES

or Modern Methods with an Antique Craft

Our pretty Lace bedroom stencils give you the option of adding as much or as little laciness to your bedroom decor as you fancy. Whole walls of lace are the ultimate but, as we show you here, 'panels' of lace look charming and original, and a narrow lace border doesn't take a minute.

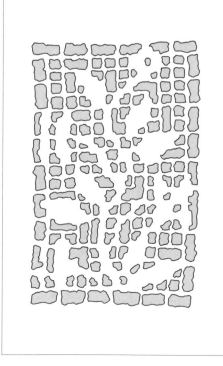

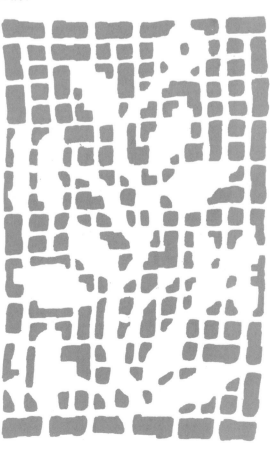

The decorative image of our Lace stencils is created in negative by clusters of lacy holes. Here the 'negative' shape is a stylised **floral spray**, which looks stunning repeated across walls.

1 We decided to keep the colour scheme simple. Lace stencils are so decorative you can keep colours understated. Here a grey-blue is used to stencil the wide lace border.

2 Join stencils on, as shown here, to create a wide lace border. A small stencil like this one should not need fastening down with masking tape. Just hold it in place with one hand.

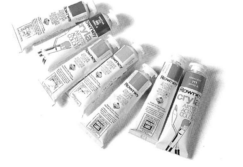

OPEN-WEAVE ART

4 The Lace flower stencil is just the same size as the wide border stencil previously shown, so it can be used from time to time to vary the design, as here. All our Lace stencils are intended to be just a tiny bit irregular, to emphasise that hand-crocheted look. Old lace is rarely mathematically regular or square.

3 One way to maximise your Lace stencils is to run the narrow lace border each side of the wider one, as here, to make a really deep band of lacy decoration which looks lovely running right round the top of your walls, below the cornice, or creating the effect of a cornice, if there isn't one.

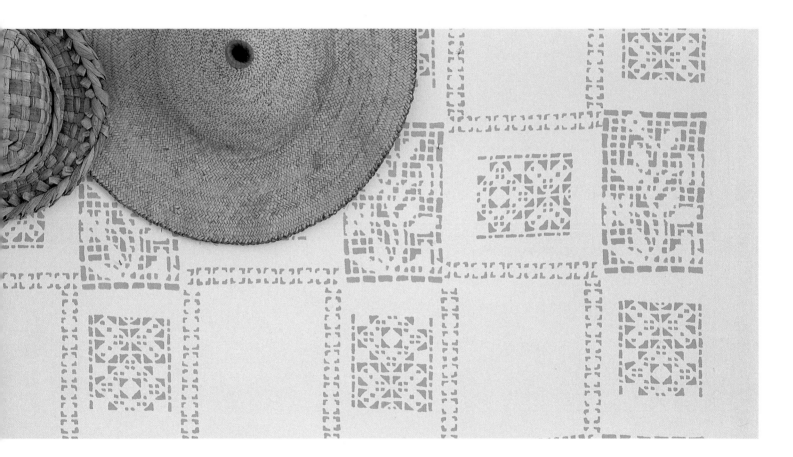

5 The Lace flower stencil on its own is superbly decorative. It looks good prettying up a simple box lid, a desk folder, even a set of lace table mats. Fasten this larger stencil down with tabs of masking tape. Use a medium artists' brush, don't overload brush with colour (test on rough paper) and paint colour through the stencil with a stippling movement for neater results.

Proving that a stencilled scheme does not have to be back-breakingly slow to make a ravishing impact on your bedroom, this simple ivory-painted room has just two lacework panels, one behind the bed, the other behind the dressing table, and our picture demonstrates how effectively this simple addition dresses up the walls. The lace motifs have been stencilled to make a repeating grid (see our photo) but a relaxed one, with no squared-off corners. Pencil or chalk guidelines before stencilling.

LAZY DAYS, LACEY NIGHTS

Bed linen is the obvious place to add the charm of traditional lace, and the effect is really special. We used the same creamy wall colour for our duvet covers and pillowcases and stencilled them in grey-blue, but here we used special fabric paints, which are washable when 'set' with a warm iron. Stencil the fabric with plastic or paper between the layers to stop the paint going through.

A touch of 'waviness' is definitely intended with our Lace stencils; to play up the 'soft' textile charm the idea is to keep to a planned grid, as here, but let the outlines meander naturally. It should *look* relaxed and delicious, as if you had fun doing it, not like a heavy-breathing geometric exercise.

A close-up showing how scrumptious a landslide of lace looks when stencilled on walls and bed linen. And it's nice to think that your stencilled efforts are real 'limited edition' stuff, your own personal creation. A low-key colour looks best for stencilling on pale shades, but on a dark or strong-coloured background you could try stencilling in plain white, or cream, or even black, for a totally different look

Spacing of lace motifs on pillowslips was done by eye, with two floral 'insertions' each side, and the narrow border emphasising the smart machined edge. On a big surface like the duvet it's best to measure and plan it out. It can help to fold it, so that you stencil a quarter of the fabric, repeating the design, each time. With these lace patterns any arrangement works.

WHY NOT LACE UP YOUR BEDROOM?

It's Attention to Detail that Makes the Difference

Keeping to the same cool, elegant, un-assertive colour scheme throughout, we show how the same set of Lace stencils can be used imaginatively to pretty up fabrics and accessories. It would be missing a trick not to have fun setting painted lace against real lace, but it's also fun to add a decorative unexpected touch of laciness to painted boxes, lamp-shades – the list is endless!

Here a simple table standing against the wall has been given a new importance by the creation of a desk-like back using all three stencil elements. Co-ordinating storage comes in the shape of simple nesting and stacking cardboard hatboxes from a department store, painted white and then stencilled with the small linking element on the edges of the lid, and the main motif displayed handsomely on the top.

The
Patchwork
Drawing Room

The Patchwork Drawing Room

'**Flower basket**' is one of the prettiest traditional Patchwork square designs, combining a pieced basket with 'appliqué' flowers, giving a nice balance between geometric and informal shapes.

'**Bow and swags**' form one of the most popular of all the quilt borders. They can be stencilled in one or two colours.

Everybody loves the crisp charm of a traditional patchwork design with squares and borders, which were used together to make heirloom quilts.

PATCH WORKS

or Decorating All Sewn Up

Sadly, antique quilts are so popular with collectors that they are hard to find and expensive, which is where our Patchwork living room stencils come in. Use them to give your home the folksy colour of traditional quilt designs.

Another old-time quilt border design with a leafier, lacier feel to it. It makes an attractive **vertical stripe** (see photo on the right).

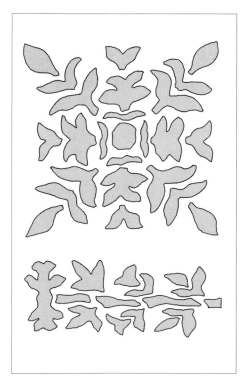

One of the handsomest and most popular of all **patchwork squares** is a design that looks well on its own or in combination with other patterns.

1 Using a cheery turkey red, a favourite colour with quilt-makers, the 'bow and swags' stencil is being painted in with a medium-sized artists' brush. Use tabs of masking tape to hold the stencil in place.

2 Repeating the 'bow and swags' motif, as shown, starts a border on its way. No problem registering this design, as bows overlap each time. Fuzzy outlines are not appropriate for quilt designs, so be careful not to pick up too much colour on your brush each time.

PATCHWORK ARTISTRY

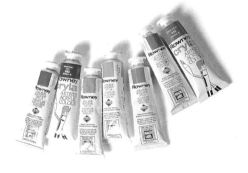

5 The other half of the flower basket has been filled with red flowers and green leaves for contrast. This design, which was popular for marriage quilts and cot quilts, also looks charming in pastel colours.

6 A new angle on the flower basket shows how many effects one stencil can lend itself to. Here the flower half of the flower basket has been doubled up to make a round motif.

3 Green and red together were favourite colour combinations on old quilts, standing out vividly against plain calico backgrounds. Stencil our 'turkey foot' in two stages, using a different brush for each colour.

4 It makes sense to stencil the basket part of the design first. A tip for tidy stencilling: stamp the loaded brush on waste paper each time to remove surplus paint.

7 The leaf border needs extra care when stencilling, like all designs with a lot of cut-outs. Tape the stencil down to hold it steady. Use a finer brush and do not let it get too wet.

8 The leaf border is best done by using the central twig shape for registering repeats. This will help you to progress much faster.

Our living room could hardly be simpler. A plain cube of a room, painted in matt creamy-white emulsion throughout. Using the Patchwork living room stencils to create 'panels' — see opposite — is a brilliant way of defining the space, throwing emphasis on a floor-length window and adding welcome colour.

STORIES FROM THE QUILT

Unremarkable furniture is transformed to match the simplest of disguises — a length of plain creamy sheeting from Russell & Chapple. To break up all this 'creaminess' we used different combinations of our Patchwork stencil designs to make some stunning cushion covers. We used warm earthy colours for our fabric stencilling, to fit in with the friendly patchwork look and to stand out well against subtle striped ticking. Quilting over these covers by machine is a quick way of giving them a lot more class.

This detailed shot shows how a panel idea works across a main wall. Keep the panels the same size and equally spaced across the wall. You will need to take measurements first, and perhaps draw out the panel arrangement first on graph paper, to find a standard panel size which will repeat across your walls without falling short of corners or overshooting them.

THE EFFECT IS SEW APPEALING

It's Attention to Detail that Makes the Difference

Traditional Patchwork designs like these have proved their perennial appeal. Their bold shapes make them natural for stencils, and of course one natural place for Patchwork stencils is on fabric — the quick modern way to treat yourself to the pleasure of looking at these delightful motifs.

Stencilled wall panels here have grown a bit to suit the wall proportions either side of a narrow door. A sturdy little bench painted and stencilled to match looks made to order for the space, and quilted cushions add the finishing touch.

A close-up shows how effectively a little machine quilting dramatises our stencilled pillow covers in subtle striped ticking. If you lack a sewing machine then a simple hand-sewn running stitch will do the job equally well, although it will take longer. The finished cushion will have a less regular but more authentically quilted look.

Our two 'patchwork cushions' show how patterns and machine quilting can be combined differently. Use polyester wadding or old blankets to quilt through. Tack the two fabrics together before machining. The tye-ends are a pretty device borrowed from pillow slips. In fact, old pillows dressed up like this make the nicest possible cushions.

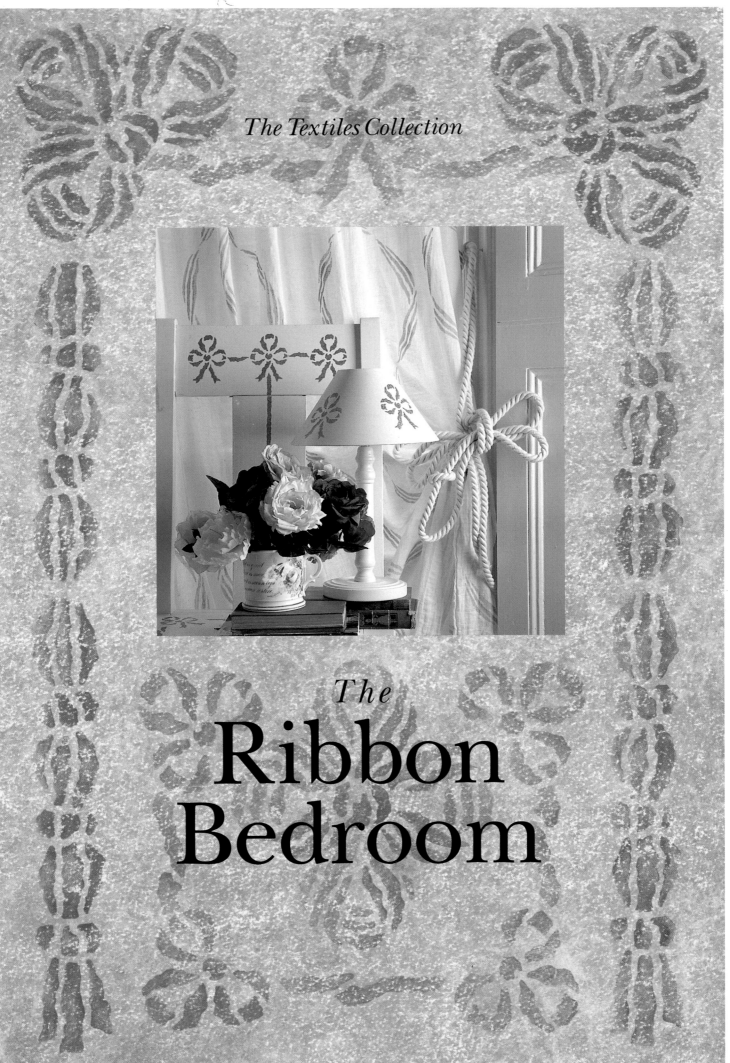

The
Ribbon
Bedroom

The
Ribbon
Bedroom

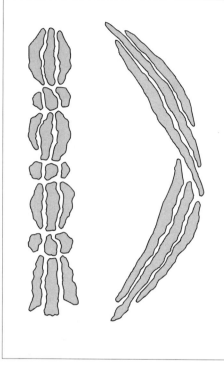

This handsome **triple bow** is the star of the Ribbon bedroom stencil collection. Use it with the bunched 'tail' to anchor pictures visually. Or with the swag to create a charming border.

This little **swag** stencil, with a half way twist, does really nice things, stencilled between triple bows. It gives a slightly Regency air to painted furniture.

All the traditional charm of ribbons and bows is in our Ribbon bedroom stencil set, but to add sparkle we have used a striped ribbon effect here and there.

RIBBONS AND BOWS

or Decorative Effects All Tied Up

With six separate stencils to play with and combine in different ways, you can really go to town on a be-ribboned bedroom. Use soft pastels for a pretty-pretty ultra-feminine look, but stronger paint colours like our soft red give a quite different jauntiness, more suggestive of military uniform cockades and medal ribbons, than fluffy boudoirs.

Small surfaces need smaller-scaled designs, so we have included a set of **mini ribbon** stencils to carry the look through to accessories and furniture.

The third element in the striped stencil set is a pretty bunched or knotted **ribbon tail**. Our pictures show lots of places where this combination works brilliantly.

Fluttering, folding **ribbon** for a miniature edition of the striped swag. It is designed to be used the same way, as part of a ribbon threesome or twosome.

This little **'tail'** supplies a useful vertical stencil element which comes in handy on chair backs and panels. See following pages for tips on combining stencils imaginatively.

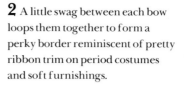

1 Use a medium artists' brush to stencil the small bow, using a stippling brush action for the neatest results. Precision matters more with small patterns, on surfaces examined close to, like furniture and accessories. Pick up colour a little at a time, testing on rough paper.

2 A little swag between each bow loops them together to form a perky border reminiscent of pretty ribbon trim on period costumes and soft furnishings.

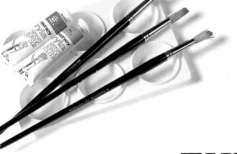

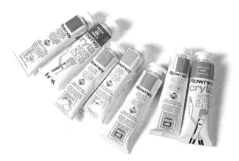

THE ART OF BOWS

4 Stencil in exactly the same way, but you may find tabs of masking tape helpful to steady the triple row while you stencil. Use the same medium brush, and minimum colour, as always, testing each time on rough paper.

5 The striped swag links two bows together. Try to keep the ends of the swag in line with the inside stripe on the bow (see the picture). This is especially important if you plan to add the bunched ribbon tail to the design, because it needs space to fit under the bow knot.

3 Stencil a 'tail' beneath each bow, and the border gains a whole new dimension. This is a dramatic shape, good for filling bigger spaces.

6 Stencil all the bows and swags first, using a pencilled guide line round a room, for instance, where the ceiling line may dip and wander (almost always in old houses). Having blocked in the border, go back and add the tails, as here.

Showing that you can't have too much of a good thing: our be-ribboned bedroom, its warm buff walls and white wood-work glamorised by our Ribbon stencil set.

TYING THE KNOT: QUIET ROMANCE

There are bows and swags on almost everything in sight, if you look closely, but the effect is not the least bit fussy or frilly. Colour choice is what sets the mood: if you want the feminine look, use pale blue or pink over antique white (what decorators call 'dirty' white; add raw umber to paint). Note how stopping the wall colour at picture rail level, and emphasising with stencils, makes a tall room seem less lofty.

Plain chairs like this used to be relegated to the bathroom or playroom, but its functional appearance has been transformed with a few stencils. Note how prettily the ribbon 'tail', doubled, draws attention to the back of the chair, and how cleverly four bows linked by mini swags 'frame' the square seat, substituting for a cushion and tying up with bows and tails on the shutter panels.

Mini bows and ribbons are a classic device for showing up the shape of furniture surfaces in a decorative way. Here a simple oak veneer bedside cupboard, given a 'limed' finish to lighten it, has been brightened with stencilling in the same red as the walls. The bunched tails and bows on the wall behind have been planned to line up with the top.

Mini bows are perfect too for dressing up room accessories effectively and quickly. Anyone at all can stencil four bows on a cheap card lampshade, but what a lot of class they add. It's the handmade touch that can make mass-produced items graciously personal. Take care to stencil crisply and clearly on an item like this: use the minimum of paint and test the brush on rough paper each time.

The final inspiration was to use the striped sway to make a lattice design stencilled on to plain creamy cotton sheeting, to make budget curtains with one-off prestige. Sheeting makes great curtains. One double-bed's width will generously drape around most windows — and it costs a great deal less than curtain fabric. Cotton cord makes an appropriate tie-back.

HINTS OF RIBBON TO FINISH

It's Attention to Detail that Makes the Difference

Most of the ideas suggested here for using your Ribbon stencils can be painted in a few minutes, but that little extra bit of time and care adds a real 'decorator' touch to a room scheme. Carrying a stencil theme through to fabrics, furniture and accessories is a pretty way of linking everything together visually, and, as our pictures show, cheap plain lampshades and painted junk furniture shoot straight upmarket.

LIST OF SOURCES AND SUPPLIERS

UNITED KINGDOM

Paint Magic Ltd

Head Office

79 Shepperton Road
Islington
London N1 3DF
tel: 0171 354 9696
fax: 0171 226 7760
mail order tel: 0171 226 4420
mail order fax: 0171 226 7760

Branches

Arundel
26 High Street
Arundel
West Sussex BN18 9AB
tel: 01903 883653
fax: 01903 884367

Belfast
59 High Street
Holywood
County Down BT18 9AQ
Northern Ireland
tel: 01232 421881
fax: 01232 421823

London
5 Elgin Crescent
Notting Hill
London W11 2JA
tel: 0171 792 8012
fax: 0171 727 0207

Richmond
116 Sheen Road
Richmond
Surrey TW9 1UR
tel: 0181 940 9799
fax: 0181 332 7503

The Stencil Store Co. Ltd

Head Office

PO Box 30
Rickmansworth
Herts WD3 5LG
tel: 01923 285577/88
fax: 01923 285136

Branches

Bath
7 Northumberland Place
Bath
BA1 5AR
tel: 01225 446528

Brighton
15c Prince Albert Street
Brighton
East Sussex
BN1 1HF
tel: 01273 721216

Bromley
79 Regent Arcade
The Glades
Bromley
Kent
tel: 0181 313 1799

Chorleywood
20-21 Heronsgate Road
Chorleywood
Herts WD3 5BN
tel: 01923 285577
(contact for details of stencilling and paint-effects work-
shops)

Kingston
Unit K3
The Bentall Centre
Wood Street
Kingston upon Thames
Surrey
tel: 0181 547 3686

London
91 Lower Sloane Street
London SW1W 8DA
tel: 0171 730 0728

Thurrock
32 Thurrock Lakeside
Shopping Centre
West Thurrock
Grays
Essex RM20 2ZF
tel: 01708 863788

York
58 Goodramgate
York
YO1 2LF
tel: 01904 640661

UNITED STATES

Paint Magic
2426 Fillmore Street
San Francisco
California 94115
tel: 415 292 7780
fax: 415 292 7782

CANADA

Paint Magic
101, 1019 17th Avenue SW
Calgary
Alberta T2T 0A7
tel: 403 245 6866
fax: 403 244 2471

SINGAPORE

Paint Magic
30 Watten Rise
Singapore 1128
tel: 65 463 1981
fax: 65 463 1982

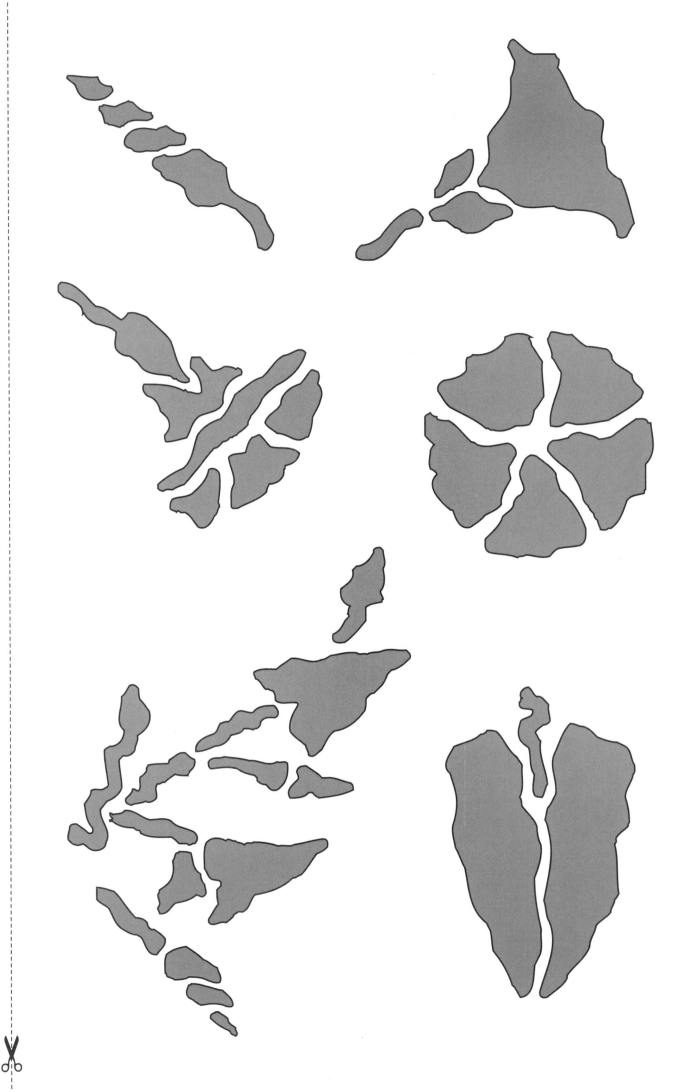

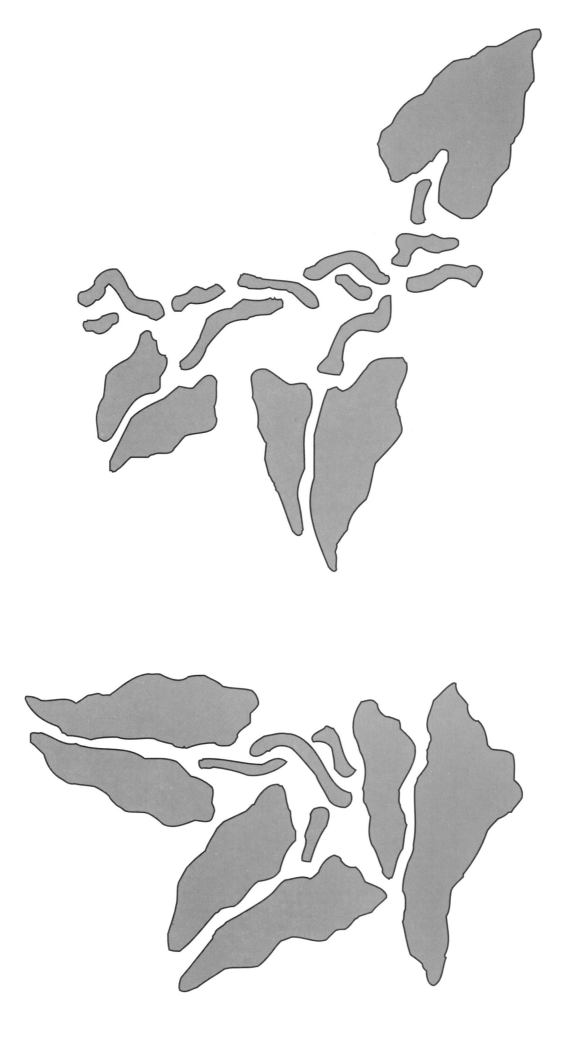

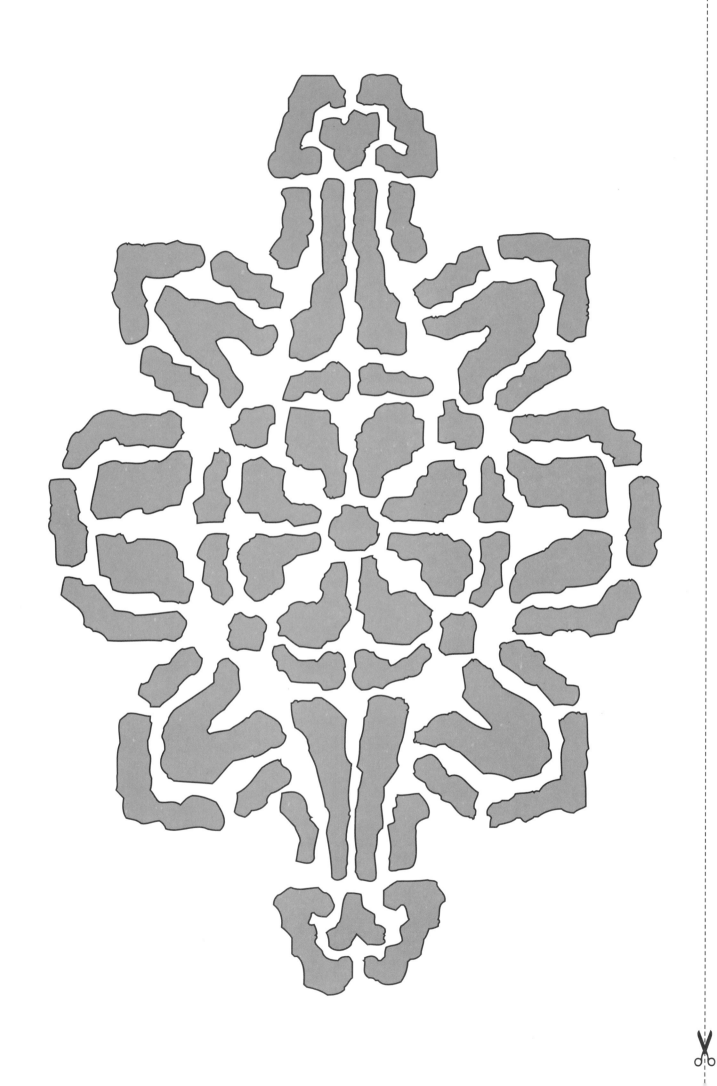

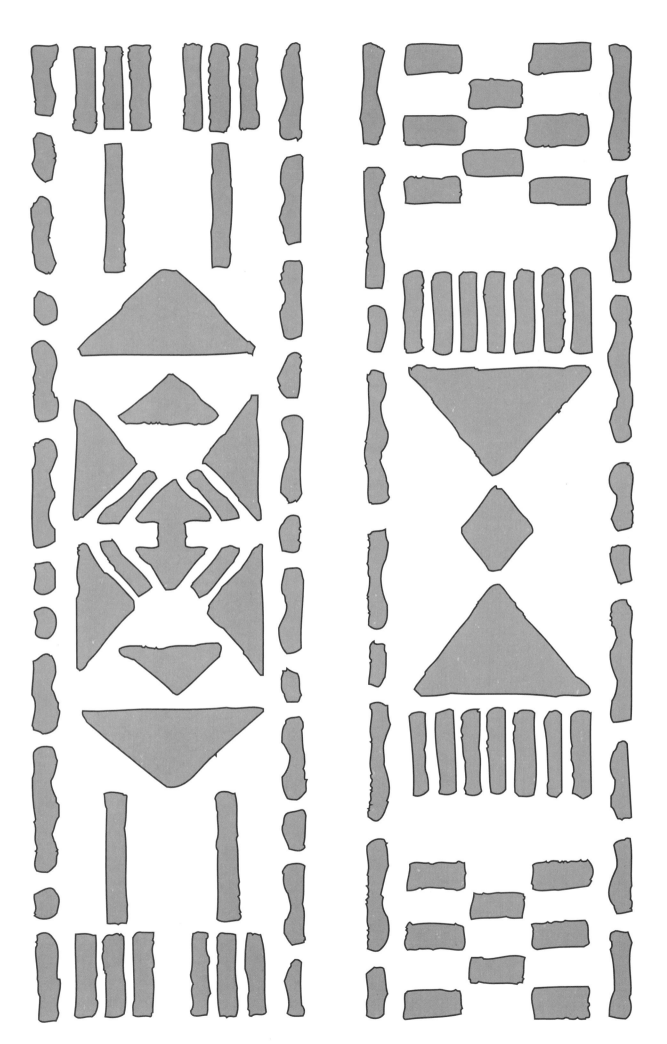

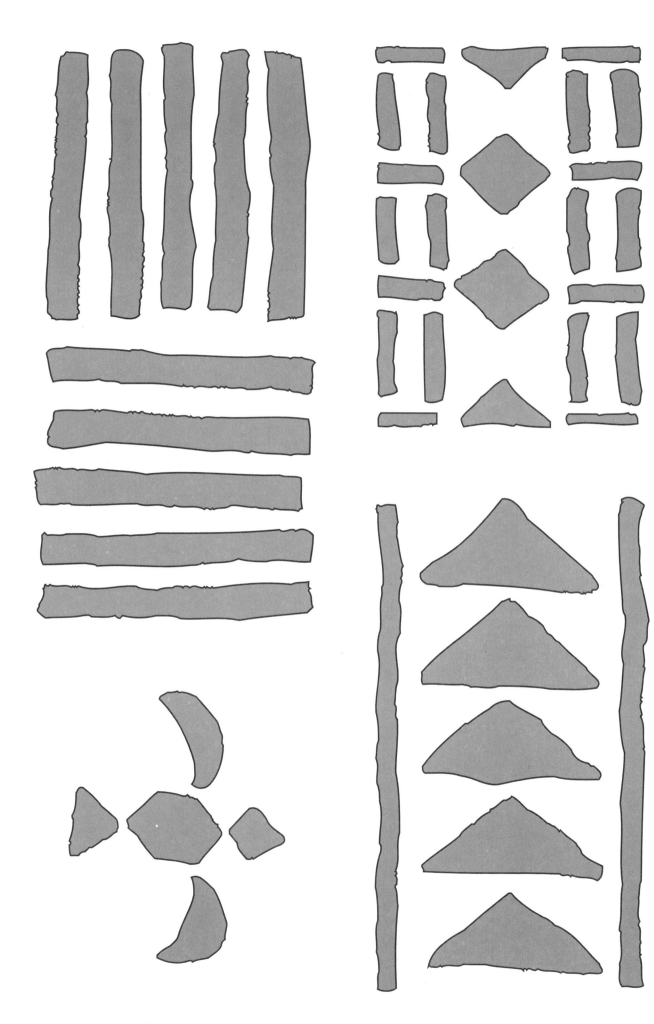

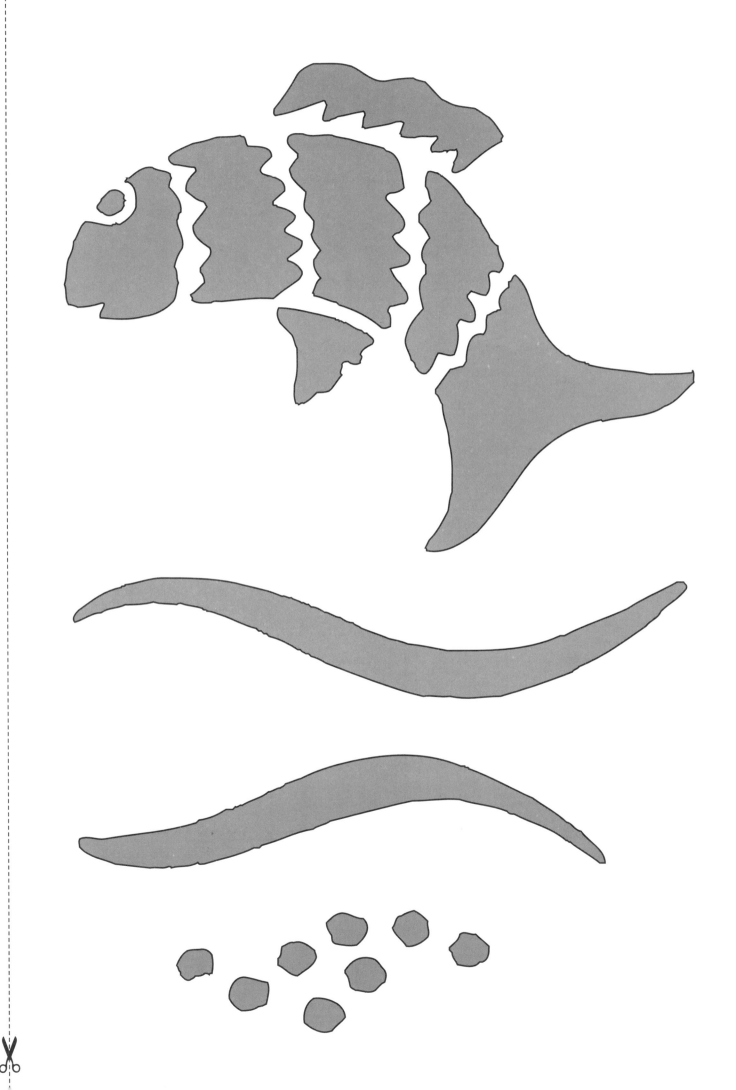

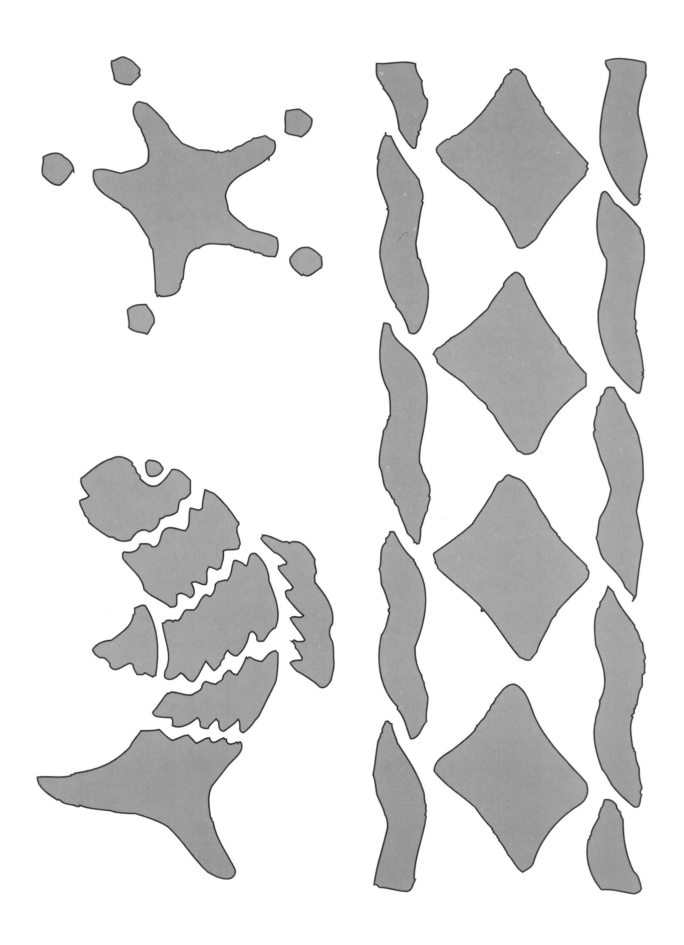

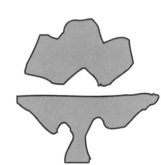

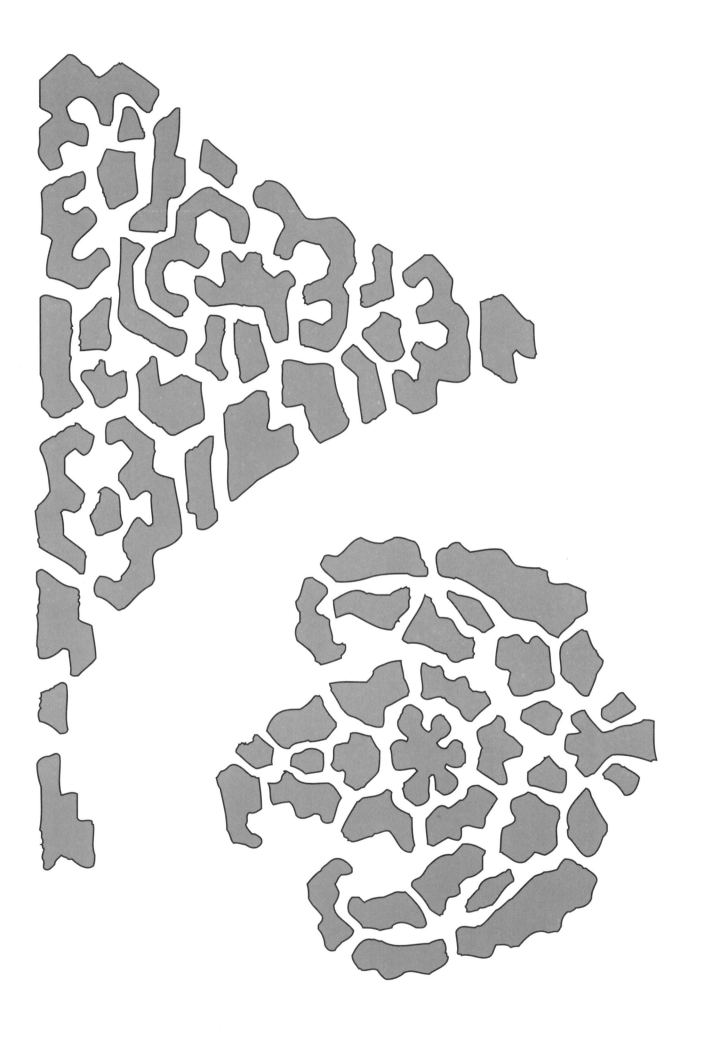

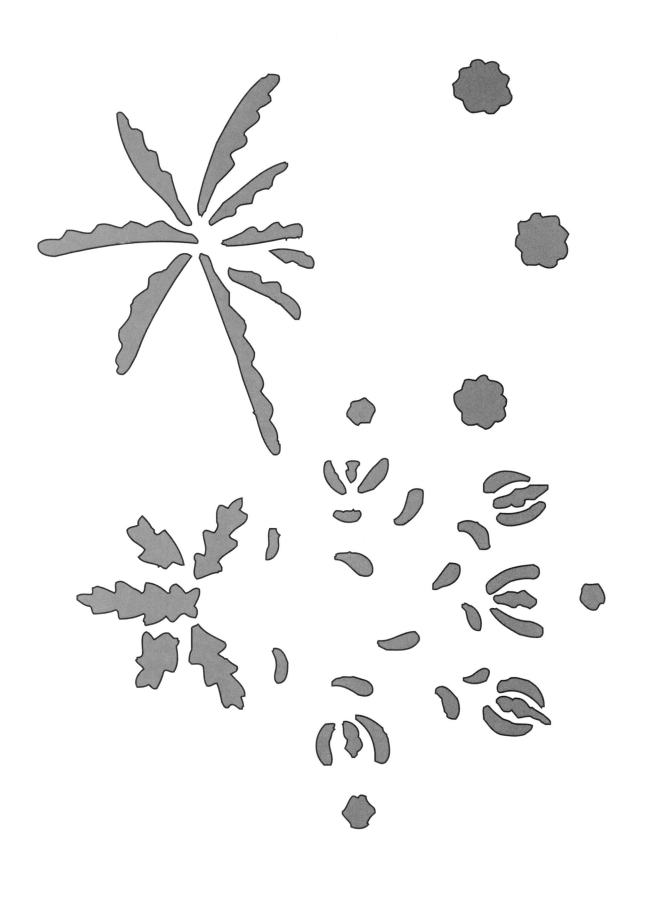

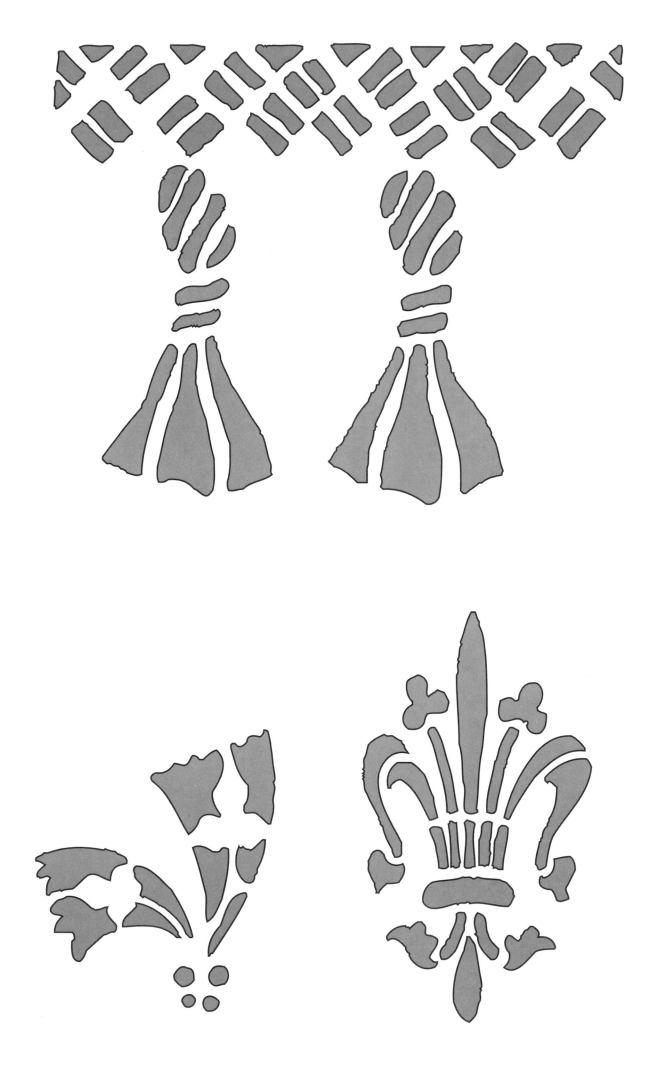

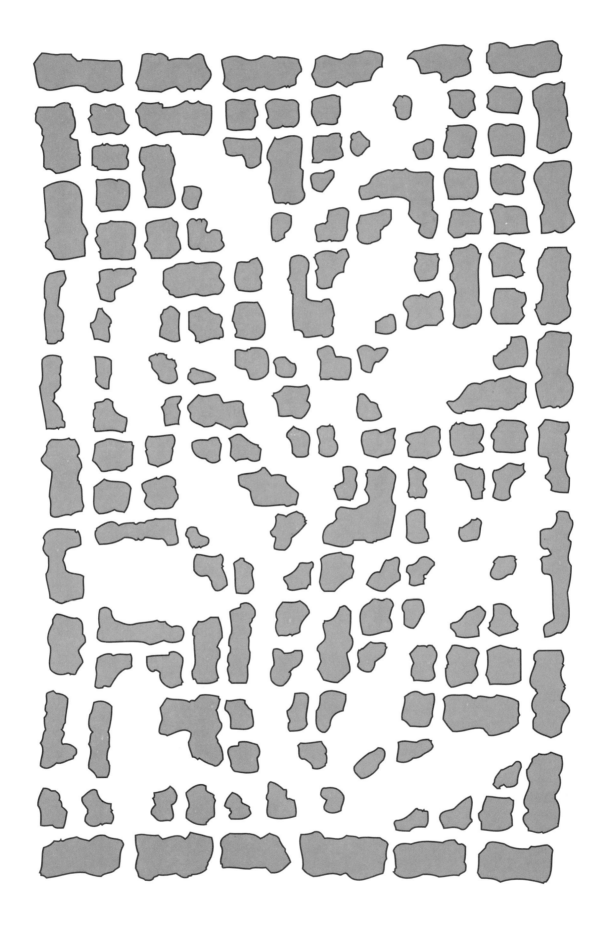

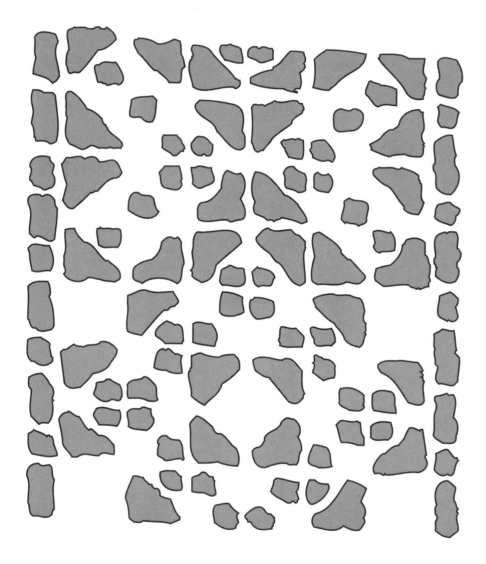

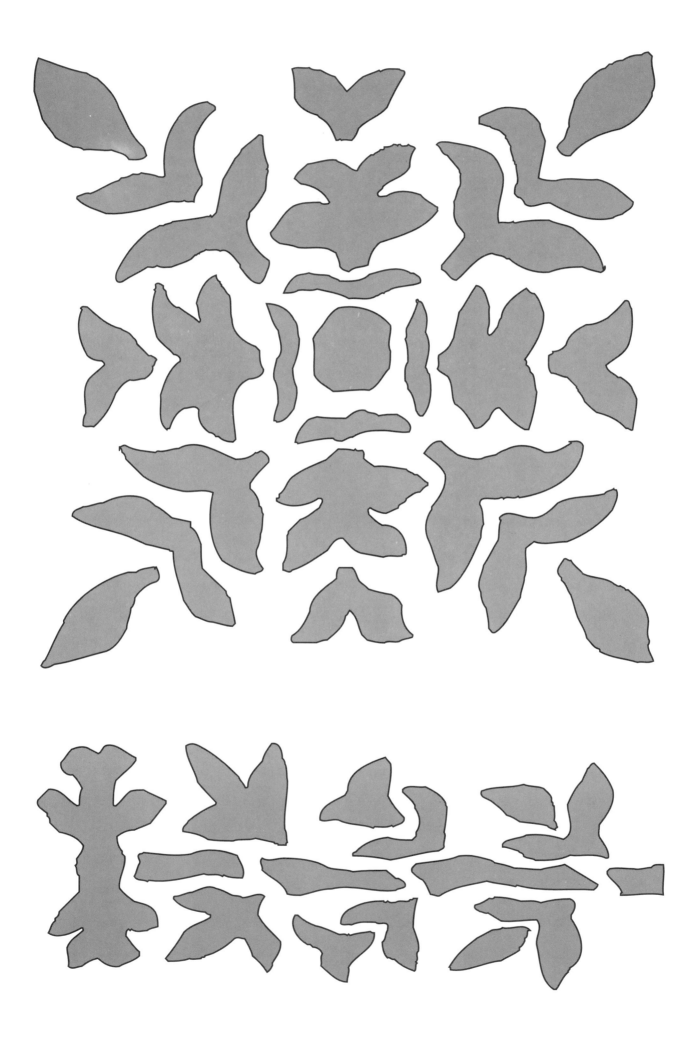

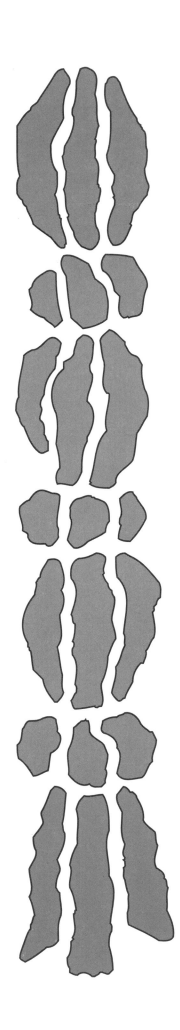

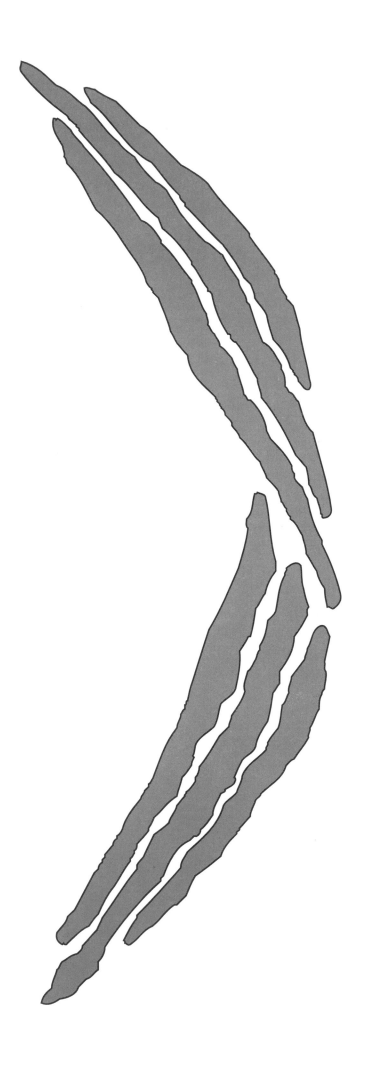